T0311919

"This short, concise but dense book has the double merit of highlighting the essential aspects of post-war French psychiatry, and of giving us the hope of seeing it re-emerge from its quasi abandonment. The book focuses on the institution François TOSQUELLES set up in its initial form at Saint-Alban: the transferential constellation. Pierre DELION defines it as "the whole diversity of people involved in caring for a patient with an archaic pathology".

The concept of "archaic pathologies" was the foothold needed to introduce the transferential relation into a context of psychosis. Its extension to archaic pathologies, in adults and in children, was implemented gradually through "multireferential transference" (TOSQUELLES) and le "dissociated transference" (Jean OURY).

In the last chapter, the author formulates five practical propositions illustrating the psychiatric professional's ethical position:

- Assuming a "desiring" position in his work.
- Ensuring the free circulation of individuals,
- thus promoting the free circulation of speech.
- Inventing made-to-measure therapeutic methods for each patient.
- Promoting relative self-management of tools needed to implement psychiatric care.

Jean-François REY, Philosophy professor, University of Lille, and expert on the history of psychiatry

Transference in Institutional Work with Psychosis and Autism

Transference in Institutional Work with Psychosis and Autism presents Pierre Delion's extensive experience in psychiatric institutions, focusing on the concept of the transferential constellation.

Delion first discusses the pioneering work of François Tosquelles at the Saint-Alban psychiatric hospital, which enabled psychoanalytic treatment to be applied in cases of severe psychopathologies. The book then explains how the transferential constellation can provide a deeper and more effective understanding of a patient's needs by engaging all caregivers within an organisation over the course of the patient's treatment history. Delion describes how regular meetings of all the team participants allow them to express different and even divergent views of the patient and to appreciate their complementary contributions to the institution. The transferential constellation is presented as an important development in the history of patient-centred psychiatric care and a touchstone for its ongoing humanistic development.

Transference in Institutional Work with Psychosis and Autism will be of great interest to psychiatrists and psychotherapists in practice and in training. It will also be key reading for other practitioners and caregivers working in mental health institutions.

Pierre Delion is a psychoanalyst and Professor Emeritus of child psychiatry at the University of Lille, France. He is the former chief of the Lille UHC Child Psychiatry Department, as well as the author of several books about babies, autism, psychosis and institutional psychotherapy.

Routledge Focus on Mental Health

Routledge Focus on Mental Health presents short books on current topics, linking in with cutting-edge research and practice.

Titles in the series:

James Joyce and the Internal World of the Replacement Child
Mary Adams

Analytic Listening in Clinical Dialogue
Basic Assumptions
Dieter Bürgin, Angelika Staehle, Kerstin Westhoff, and Anna Wyler von Ballmoos

Treatment for Body-Focused Repetitive Behaviors
An Integrative Psychodynamic Approach
Stacy K. Nakell

Psychoanalysis and the Act of Artistic Creation
A Look at the Unconscious Dynamics of Creativity
Luís Manuel Romano Delgado

Technology in Mental Health
Foundations for Clinical Use
Jessica Stone

Transference in Institutional Work with Psychosis and Autism
The Transferential Constellation
Pierre Delion
Translated by Agnès Jacob

For a full list of titles in this series, please visit www.routledge.com/ Routledge-Focus-on-Mental-Health/book-series/RFMH

Transference in Institutional Work with Psychosis and Autism

The Transferential Constellation

Pierre Delion

Translated by Agnès Jacob

Routledge
Taylor & Francis Group

LONDON AND NEW YORK

First published 2023
by Routledge
4 Park Square, Milton Park, Abingdon, Oxon OX14 4RN

and by Routledge
605 Third Avenue, New York, NY 10158

Routledge is an imprint of the Taylor & Francis Group, an informa business

British Library Cataloguing-in-Publication Data
A catalogue record for this book is available from the British
Library

ISBN: 978-1-032-46148-9 (hbk)
ISBN: 978 1-032-46147-2 (pbk) (NIP)
ISBN: 978-1-003-38026-9 (ebk)

DOI: 10.4324/9781003380269

Typeset in Times New Roman
by Apex CoVantage, LLC

To Jeanne, Joseph,
Capucine, Gabrielle and Marin

Contents

Introduction

We are living in an era which will gradually render the psychoanalytic concept of transference invisible. Psychiatry, under the influence of powerful lobbies primarily representing the fields of genetics and neurosciences, and aided by government policies aimed at short-term cost cuts, while at the same time public health care is unscrupulously sold to the private sector, is in danger of rapidly becoming dehumanised and setting aside the lessons of its complex history, which has nevertheless allowed us to understand that the sources of mental illness are linked to multiple bio-psycho-social factors. While psychopathological and social factors are better understood today, undeniable advances in genetics and the neurosciences are received with great interest, but should never become the only factors taken into account. If this were to happen, we would risk seeing the emergence of psychiatry without a subject – quasi veterinary – with scientific premises rooted in evidence-based medicine (EBM) – quite the opposite of Jacques Schotte's proposition[1] of anthropopsychiatry. This EBM-style psychiatry would ignore the importance of intersubjective relations and of social context in the treatment of patients. And what would become of transferential relations, which would certainly continue to exist but would be excluded from our therapeutic panoply?

Yet this concept is undoubtedly one of the most crucial in psychiatry, thanks to the discoveries of Freudian psychopathology. Freud's invention of this brilliant notion still helps us to understand and treat "ordinary" neurosis in the Western world. Unfortunately, the concept of neurosis has become obsolete in official psychiatric usage, which is now determined by the international classification of the DSM-5. "Neurosis" has been replaced by "disorder", a notion that has lost all psychoanalytic connotation. Yet the psychopathology of neuroses made it possible to search for the meaning of the different symptoms it "embodied", allowing patients to become participants in this research. This dispensed them from having to take addictive anxiolytics and/or antidepressants, highly recommended by the reasoning underlying the new classifications. Often, when they are prescribed in the absence of any psychotherapeutic work conducted in parallel, the only result is chemical anesthesia that numbs desire and its expression.

Metapsychological investigations were needed to extend the understanding and the therapeutic effects of transference to *archaic pathologies*,[2] and in particular to psychoses. They too, like the neuroses, have gradually been displaced by a catalogue of observable behaviours requiring the prescription of neuroleptics, the use of a therapeutic technique and recourse to behavioural therapies, but leaving out any psychopathological perspective.

We have even seen that in regard to children the concept of psychosis has been eliminated from the new classifications, to the great relief of detractors of psychoanalysis, on the pretext that this designation would justify the intervention of a . . . psychiatrist. Pervasive developmental disorders, replaced in the DSM-5 by Autism Spectrum Disorders (ASD), have definitively left the sphere of psychiatry since from now on paediatric neurologists are authorised to treat them, although many of them have no experience with the long-term day-to-day management of neurodevelopmental disorders, of which ASDs are emblematic and autism is the most representative spectrum.

Let us remember that precocious infantile autism and depression in children, described in 1943 by Leo Kanner and René Spits respectively, contributed greatly to the creation of child psychiatry. Not surprisingly, therefore, what is at stake is the survival of child psychiatry itself.

We no longer speak of child archaic pathologies, according to the French classification proposed by Roger Misès, which grouped together infantile psychoses and developmental disharmonies in children unable to establish transferential relations, as Freud so aptly described them in his work on neurosis. All those who have worked with these children know from experience that transferential relations with them exist, but develop in a manner different than those associated with neurosis. Indeed, these children do not form object relations as they were described by the first psychoanalysts. And, above all, from the psychopathological perspective, certain adult pathologies, with schizophrenia ranking first, share the same characteristics. Although many of Freud's disciples attempted to treat archaic pathologies in children and adults using standard analytic treatment, we must admit that their results were mediocre.[3] August Aichhorn (1878–1949) might be an exception, since he achieved some success in re-educating "abandoned" youth in Austria. In addition, Harry Stack Sullivan[4] and Frieda Fromm-Reichmann in the United States, among a few other practitioners, treated psychotic patients successfully.

But when Tosquelles proposed that the metapsychology of transference be re-examined in the context of these pre-objectal stage pathologies, insisting on the need for the institution as the missing link in their management, a new threshold was crossed in the domain of transferential psychopathologies, and the teachings of psychoanalysis could once again make a useful contribution. Joyce McDougal, a great psychoanalyst of the 20th century, stressed the importance of "reshaping the metapsychology with each new patient".

The transferential constellation is the outcome of this crucial development in the management of archaic pathologies; it is correlated with the invention of institutional psychotherapy.

This book will attempt to present a comprehensive picture of this fundamental concept which makes it possible to offer psychiatric treatment to children and adults presenting these serious pathologies, in accordance with a transferential psychopathological perspective.

Notes

1 Schotte, J., *Vers l'anthropopsychiatrie*, Paris: Hermann, 2008.
2 I propose that we define "archaic pathologies" as those affecting children and adults who remain in a world of partial objects, without being able to arrive at a total object in a stable manner. These pathologies include mainly autism, the psychoses and schizophrenia. But borderline pathologies, disharmonies with a psychotic structure, certain types of emotional deprivation and addictions can legitimately be considered archaic pathologies as well.
3 Roudinesco, E., *Freud in His Time and Ours*, Cambridge, MA: Harvard University Press, 2016.
4 Sullivan, H.S., *Schizophrenia as a Human Process*, New York: W.W. Norton, 1981.

Chapter 1

The Concept of Transference in Neurosis and Psychosis

Laplanche and Pontalis define transference in psychoanalysis as "a process through which unconscious desires are displaced onto certain objects in the context of a certain type of relation established with them", which is the case in the analytic relation. What occurs in the transference is "the repetition of unconscious infantile patterns reactivated and intensely felt to be lived in the present".[1] As psychoanalysis began to take shape, Freud observed the phenomenon of transference when Anna O.'s cathartic treatment with Joseph Breuer failed. It was then that Freud abandoned hypnosis. At the start of the 20th century, Dora's psychoanalysis was one of the first psychoanalytic experiences involving a person presenting a case of hysterical neurosis. For Freud, this case was very instructive as to the difficulties of "handling transference in neurosis". Later, in 1914, in *Remembering, Repeating, Working-through*, Freud introduced the concept of transference neurosis, which causes the patient to repeat in the transference his childhood conflicts. In 1920, he specified that:

> in the sphere of transference . . . the earlier neurosis has been replaced by a fresh "transference neurosis" . . . : to force as much as possible into the channel of memory and to allow as little as possible to emerge as repetition.[2]

But Freud and his followers continued to encounter numerous problems inherent to transference phenomena in the course of the analytic encounter, involving both patients and practitioners, and extending to the ensuing work of theorisation. Thus, transference shifted from being seen as a type of resistance in the treatment to being a fundamental

DOI: 10.4324/9781003380269-1

factor needed to carry it out, in certain ethical conditions. Like Freud and Ferenczi, we can define transference as:

> a process constituting an element of the analytic cure, through which the unconscious desires of the analyst and with regard to the external objects are transferred, in this context, onto the analyst, who is put in the position of one to whom these objects can be brought..[3]

In his teaching, Lacan considers transference one of the four fundamental concepts of psychoanalysis and defines it as: "the actualization of unconscious fantasies, memories and wishes during psychoanalytic treatment".[4]

The neurotic patient who came to see Freud told his own story with relative coherence. He was able to compose a narrative of his life. This allowed him to speak about things he considered problematic or absurd – slips of the tongue, nightmares, self-sabotaging behaviour, neurotic symptoms . . . trying to understand them as the present expression of an unconscious language reflecting his childhood story brought back by "free association" of ideas and memories in the course of the sessions. Thus, he is the narrator of his own existence.

A schizophrenic, however, cannot produce such a narration. If asked to tell his story, he has difficulty doing so or cannot do it at all. And if you go to the trouble of putting something together for him – a narrative – you are no further advanced. Sometimes he will say: "Yes, that's me", but if he is dissociated, he might insist that he never told you any of these things. In that case, you are the one who is confused by the schizophrenic. His narrative is not coherent, there is no stable thread that would enable him to say: "I say something in the first person, and I inscribe it in my story". No, what he says is not inscribed. His discourse remains outside of common sense. Such a person can say very intelligent things – Antonin Artaud made brilliant speeches, but from time to time, when he was caught up in his delusion, what he said lost all internal coherence. The schizophrenic's speech is not a stable system; it is constantly being reshaped. Therefore, he cannot build his existence around it.

Yet there is transference: the patient meets a caregiver and has an outpouring of emotion towards him, a desire to be near him, to hold on to him; or this person provokes an outburst of hate; often, the patient has ambivalent emotions – what used to be called "affects" in the Freudian era – towards the caregiver. But all this is not expressed in ordinary interpersonal relations based on our usual social code.

The schizophrenic has an open-air unconscious. In the transference with him, caregivers have to take things as they come and attempt to put them together, to connect them in a narrative.

Indeed, the role of the caregiver consists, as Jacques Hochmann reminds us, drawing his inspiration from Paul Ricoeur,[5] of creating a narrative. If the patient who is asked to tell his story recognises himself in the narrative the caregiver puts together for him, he will feel better because the caregiver performed a holding function which made him feel supported – phoric function – and recognised, in part. This can be described as a kind of mirror stage through narration.

In effect, the narrative is constructed in the absence of symptoms in the relation with caregivers. In the patient's daily life, impulsive acts occur; the caregiver, instead of seeing them as elements of an as-yet-enigmatic language to decipher, is too often busy watching him closely to "prevent" these events from happening. He then writes on the observation chart that the patient is uncontrollable, even dangerous, and that his medication should be increased, when in fact the patient is struggling with archaic fears. The accumulation of such "targeted transmissions" unfortunately often results in "iatrogenic" acting out in retaliation. The problem with the new psychiatry is the increased risk of focusing on behaviour only and ignoring what it tries to signify.

A patient wants to go out of his hospital pavillion to smoke a cigarette. The caretaker who can give him permission has a lot of work to finish before being able to go with him. Two hours later, the patient comes back and asks to go out and smoke again. The caregiver still can't give him permission. The patient becomes aggressive with the caregiver, who then threatens him with being put in restraints because of his aggression. A few minutes later, his violent behaviour does, in fact, lead to the use of restraints. After this "incident", the caregiver, depressed, tells his colleagues, "I didn't choose to work with people to end up doing this! If we had more personnel, this patient would never have been restrained". Later, when he met with the hospital occupational physician, he complained that his work had lost meaning for him and that he was thinking of doing something else. No narrative was created, since what happened did not follow ethical rules but was instead only an arrangement based on visible behaviour. The patient's violent acting out in response to institutional violence could have acquired meaning in an exact account of what took place.

Conversely, institutional psychotherapy, in addition to granting great importance to the patients' freedom to come and go freely, strives to gradually create a narrative of interpersonal experiences. This is what

Jean Oury meant to say when he proposed to transform impulsive acts into acting out; that is, to understand them in the context of a transferential relation rather than as isolated acts without meaning.[6] In this perspective, the caregivers are constant witnesses to the patients' discontinuous experiences, and the creation of a narrative consists of establishing continuity where discontinuity reigns. To do this, the caregivers must be considered subjects in their own right — that is, interlocutors for the patients — rather than merely interchangeable people who are there to check that patients take their medication, or to supervise them and, if need be, to punish them.[7] The training caregivers receive should prepare them to accept and deal with psychotic transference, or, as Gisela Pankow[8] said, accept to descend into hell with them.

This vision of institutional psychotherapy, and more specifically of the transferential constellation, is founded on a psychopathological understanding of transference and its manifestations, particularly in archaic pathologies. This philosophy of work must be translated into a therapeutic strategy developed with all the actors involved.

Notes

1 Laplanche, J., Pontalis, J.-B., *The Language of Psychoanalysis*, Paris: W.W. Norton, 1974.
2 Freud, S., "Beyond the Pleasure Principle", *S.E.*, 18, London: Hogarth.
3 Roudinesco, E., Plon, M., "Transfert", in *Dictionnaire de la psychanalyse*, Paris: Livrepoche, 2011.
4 Lacan, J., *The Seminar of Jacques Lacan*, Book XI, Miller, J.-A. (ed.), New York: W.W. Norton, 1998.
5 Ricoeur, P., *Time and Narrative*, Chicago: University of Chicago Press, 1990.
6 It is in this light that semiotic research reveals its importance. On this subject, see Michel Balat, *Fondements sémiotiques de la psychanalyse*, Paris: L'Harmattan, 2000.
7 Foucault, M., *Discipline and Punish*, New York: Vintage Books, 1995.
8 Gisela Pankow (1914–1998), French psychoanalyst of German origin, specialised in psychosis.

Chapter 2

Multireferential Transference and the Institution

When I first knew François Tosquelles, he told me a story that made it very easy for me to understand how he proposed to extend Freud's concept of transference. It was, in fact, a question of understanding the specificity of psychosis and of developing a metapsychology of transference that takes it into account.

A man with schizophrenic symptoms comes to the Pere Mata Hospital in Reus (Catalonia) to be hospitalised, as his family doctor has advised him to do. He is greeted by the hospital janitor, who asks how he can help him. The patient has a good feeling about the janitor and starts to talk to him about his problems in his job as a roofer, about voices he hears when he is on rooftops, and about the unkind remarks of his roofing craftsman boss. The janitor, not used to being entrusted with such confidences, listens with curiosity and great humanity. After these initial revelations which indicate the man's distress, the janitor tells him that "he is only the janitor" and offers to take him to see a nurse he knows who will tell him what he can do to feel better. He takes him to the admissions office and introduces him to the nurse, telling the patient he was very happy to meet him and that he is at his disposal if there is anything else he can do. The patient thanks him very warmly and the nurse takes over from there. He also has a good feeling about her and proceeds to tell her about his marital problems, his wife's reluctance to accept that the voices he hears are real, and his disagreements with his oldest son. . . . After a while, the nurse announces that he has to be seen by the head of the hospital's Psychiatric Department, who will diagnose him and recommend treatment. The patient makes sure that he will still be able to talk to the nurse, who is sympathetic like the janitor was. As soon as the patient catches a glimpse of the psychiatrist, who agrees to see him in his office, he tells the nurse that the doctor "gives him a bad feeling" and that he doesn't want to see him. The nurse insists, saying

DOI: 10.4324/9781003380269-2

that she has worked with this doctor for a long time, and that he is very competent. The patient agrees to go into the office, sits down, and the psychiatrist starts the interview. But the patient, who keeps looking at the ground, doesn't answer any of his questions and is very reluctant to respond to the doctor's attempts at making contact.

Tosquelles ended his narrative at that point and asked me how this situation could be used to suggest a diagnosis and treatment. I tried to find an answer based on the little I knew at the time. He then went ahead and told me that this situation could be looked at from two very different psychiatric perspectives: one, of which he did not approve but had seen applied in many different situations, seemed to him to be a 19th century practice specific to the functioning of asylums; and another, which had emerged from his encounters with others, particularly psychoanalysts, and which led him to conceive of an innovative form of psychiatry. The first form of psychiatry is based on the opinion of the psychiatrist who sees the patient, and pays insufficient attention to the environment "he brings with him". This patient does not speak during the first session. He seems reluctant and is probably experiencing hallucinations. His rigid posture suggests a catatonic state. He must be hospitalised since he is probably psychotic.

But if the second perspective guides the psychiatric work, the psychiatrist observes the patient's clinical state in his office, but he speaks to the nurse to ask for her opinion since she is the one who asked him to see the patient quickly to hospitalise him. Her opinion is very different than his, and he quickly realises that the diagnosis he was likely to make would have been based on insufficient information. Moreover, the nurse tells him that the janitor accompanied the patient to the admissions office, and that he and the patient seemed to be in remarkably close terms. The psychiatrist asks the nurse and the janitor to meet with him, and each of them tells him what happened when they met the patient.

Tosquelles draws two essential conclusions.

The first concerns what he initially called "multireferential transference", to describe the different forms of transference – different than those with neurotic patients – that the patient establishes with each person he meets. Later, Tosquelles would explain that objects and spaces can also be invested in the transference. Claude Poncin's medical thesis, written in Saint-Alban in 1963, is very instructive in this regard, since it proposes that the "situem" be considered a spatial equivalent of the "phonem" and the "monem", and that the spaces where psychotic patients are treated be submitted to a "structural analysis applied to institutional psychotherapy". In the same perspective, what would be called

Brut Art by Dubuffet a few years later – something Oury was interested in during his internship at Saint-Alban – was seen by Tosquelles as one of the knowable effects of object investment by some schizophrenics. His closeness with Auguste Forestier clearly influenced many of his clinical observations.[1]

The second important outcome of the Pere Mata Hospital story was the invention of the transferential constellation meeting, to take into account multireferential transference.

Reading the example given by Tosquelles makes it easy to understand multireferential transference. Here we have a schizophrenic patient who, depending on who he meets, will talk about aspects of his life that, being partial elements, cannot constitute a coherent reason explaining his presence at the hospital. To the first two people he meets, who represent good partial objects (Klein), he talks about things he believes will interest each of them; the janitor, a man, will be interested in his work and in the problems related to his job, while the nurse, a woman, will be interested in his marital troubles and his problems with his son. When he meets the third person, the psychiatrist, he immediately takes him to be a hostile person so he keeps silent and takes on the demeanour of one who is persecuted. These three people encountered while he is on his way to be hospitalised are embodiments of his relations with his partial objects. The transference is multireferential. This first fundamental step towards a new perspective was followed by another, just as crucial, created by Oury: the concept of "dissociated transference".

Thus, Tosquelles was determined to take this observation seriously, rather than think, as it was still usual to do at the time, that only the psychoanalyst could act as the recipient of the patient's transference. He insisted on the need for an institution – in this case, the transferential constellation – that could accommodate and treat a psychotic person who "transferred partially" on the three people he met: the janitor, the nurse and the psychiatrist.

The Freudian device of traditional analysis alone is not suited to patients presenting these archaic pathologies. Given that a group of professionals is needed to care for a psychotic person, it is useful to regard this set of people as an institution. Tosquelles specifies that we must not confuse the establishment with the institution in order to not lose sight of the true importance of the latter. In his view, the establishment is created by the State to carry out missions according to laws created by democratically elected bodies. Thus, schools, colleges and academies are establishments, as are hospitals. The first serve to educate children, while the second are intended to provide care to citizens. But we all know that depending on the individuals who fill the positions in each establishment, results can be very different. The term "institution" is reserved for the totality of the people who allow the establishment to fulfill its missions. Therefore, it is important to consider the institution as the human form taken by an establishment to carry out missions set by the laws of a country.

When Tosquelles concludes that an institution is needed to look after and treat psychotic persons who enter into specific forms of transference with the professionals who work with them, he is defining what is needed to treat a particular pathology. He draws his inspiration from surgeons who need aseptic conditions to operate on their patients. In psychiatry, to treat archaic pathologies, there must be a diversity of people engaged in the collective enterprise he calls the "institution".

And the paradigmatic form of an institution is the transferential constellation. Within it, a number of rules have to be followed to optimise the care offered to patients.

- First, the members of the institution have to meet regularly to recount their experiences with the patients assigned to them.
- In addition, these meetings facilitate and encourage honest expression to allow the narration of these experiences without concerns about hierarchical positions. Viewpoints can be contradictory, and no one will be in a position to say that someone's narrative of what he experienced is more important than someone else's.
- Lastly, the content of the meetings will not be used outside the context of the treatment of the patient discussed. Once the caregivers have accepted these conditions, regardless of their status, the concept of transferential constellation acquires all its usefulness in the management of psychotic patients.

In more general terms, this initial institutional form can be followed by other types of institutions that can complete the approach to the treatment of those afflicted with mental illness. For instance, a therapeutic club, the production of a newspaper, the organising of cultural activities, are all opportunities to bring patients together with caregivers and to transform the management of these patients into an active process.

Tosquelles often referred to a book by Hermann Simon, a psychiatrist in Gütersloh, Germany, in which the author stressed the need to treat the entropy of the hospital before undertaking to treat patients, and to do so specifically by giving the latter an active role in their own care.

Institutional psychotherapy is simply the possibility given to a team of caregivers and to patients to organise themselves in order to carry out together a treatment process – psychotherapy – by relying on institutions.[2] In this perspective, the meeting is the key concept of the undertaking, since it is seen as the condition allowing the concerted design of individual therapy, helped by reliance on groups and institutions.

Notes

1 Cf. Tosquelles holding one of Auguste Forestier's boats at arm's length on the roof of the Saint-Alban castle (L'Aracine Brut Art collection).
2 Michaud, G., *La Borde, un pari nécessaire. De la notion d'institution à la psychothérapie institutionnelle*, Preface by F. Tosquelles, Paris: Gauthier-Villars, 1977.

Chapter 3

Dissociated Transference in Adult Patients

Jean Oury, the founder of the La Borde clinic, completed part of his intern-ship in Saint-Alban between 1947 and 1949. He was to become one of the inventors of institutional psychotherapy, along with Tosquelles and a few others. This innovative and highly cultured thinker – an important figure in contemporary psychiatry – suggested that Tosquelles could enrich the concept of multireferential transference by including the crucial advances made by Eugene Bleuler, psychiatrist at the Burghölzi clinic in Zurich. Bleuler found that the designation "*dementia praecox*", invented by Emil Kraepelin in reference to the work of his colleague Alzheimer on prese-nile dementia, was poorly suited to his conception of this form of psy-chosis. He therefore coined the term "schizophrenia"[1] to replace it. He considered the schizophrenic process to originate in a primary symptom: dissociation (*Spaltung* in German). In his 1908 article preceding the pub-lication of his book in 1911, he referred to the *Spaltung* in these terms:

> I believe that the tearing apart [*die Zerreissung*] or splitting [*die Spaltung*] of psychic functions is a prominent symptom of the whole group.[2] . . . From the psychological viewpoint, the greatest problem seems to be a loosening of associations. In schizophrenia, it is as if inhibitions and physiological processes have lost their meaning. The usual paths are no longer followed, the thread of ideas is easily lost in unfamiliar and misleading detours. Associations become tributary to haphazard influences, and especially to emotions. All this leads to the more or less complete disappearance of logical reasoning. In periods of crisis, associations are broken up into small pieces, so that despite the fact that psychomotor behaviour is unaffected, no action is pos-sible because no thought is followed through, and a variety of con-tradictory impulses subsist side by side, with no possibility of being synthesized into a unified emotional or intellectual point of view.

DOI: 10.4324/9781003380269-3

In his 1911 work, Bleuler proposed the following definition:

> The splitting [*Spaltung*] is the prerequisite condition of most of the complicated phenomena of the disease; it gives [its] peculiar stamp to the entire symptomatology. But underneath this systematic fragmentation into established sets of ideas, we find a primal disintegration of the associative structure, which can lead to an irregular fragmentation [*Zerspaltung*] of such solidly established elements as concrete ideas. The term "schizophrenia" refers to both kinds of splitting which often fuse in their effects.[3]

Alain Bottéro, who documented the history of the concept of dissociation, provided the following clarification in the current nosology:

> Through dissociation, Bleuler went from the symptoms of incurable intellectual and moral deterioration to compensation by a psyche with a relaxed associative capacity, unable to set in motion the different forces involved in affectivity. This new understanding of symptoms considered incomprehensible opened the way to a psychotherapeutic approach to the treatment of the most severely affected psychiatric patients.[4]

Bottéro was able to apply this approach himself in the Burghölzi clinic in Zurich.

But what are the principles guiding the practice of today's psychiatrists? And what are psychiatrists in training taught about schizophrenia?

Bleuler/EY or the DSM-5? Singularity or Statistical Logic?

Two very different perspectives oppose each other: Bleuler's (translated into French by Henri Ey), which was predominant throughout the second half of the 20th century; and that of the DSM-5, which has become dominant in the past few years. I believe it is useful to present them both. In fact, Bleuler's perspective should continue to guide clinical practice, while the DSM-5 (Diagnostic and Statistical Manual) should provide statistical results to researchers, since it classifies the signs of mental illness based on criteria related mainly to incidence. The DSM-5 is in no way a clinical psychiatric manual although, despite this, it has indeed become a manual under cover of a so-called scientific approach.

The clinical session can now be replaced by the filling out of grids, giving the patient or his family the impression of taking part in a scientific project. The latter, perfectly legitimate within the framework of certified research, can in no way replace actual interpersonal exchanges in the course of a session.

But statistical reasoning has nevertheless taken the lead.[5] In the fight against smoking or against motor vehicle accidents, biostatisticians can assert that based on their data, above a certain quantity of tobacco or a certain speed at the wheel, there is a calculable risk of pathology in the first case, and of an accident in the second.

Based on conclusions drawn from this, biopower intends to modify our behaviour using biostatistics and prevention. But we can give counter-examples that put these modern facts in perspective, because each human subject also has a singularity which distances him from the Gaussian mean. Indeed, Gauss calculated and defined a normal curve to describe statistical findings scientifically. Keeping these singularities in mind, and given that their number increases the farther they are from the peak of the curve, care must be taken not to apply statistical findings to mental health without taking precautions. So much the better if statistics can help in the prevention of lung cancer and motor vehicle accidents, but the same reasoning cannot justify using them as the sole basis for treatment in psychiatry.

Although statistical reasoning is only one aspect of scientific logic, medical reasoning is not the equivalent of scientific reasoning. When a child is brought to see me for a consultation, my ethical obligation cannot be subjected to scientific simplification and cannot be based solely on the logic of science. Statistics are useful as information that can guide the decision, within a medical relation which must take into account many other criteria. Science itself cannot be reduced to statistical reasoning: a beautifully formulated mathematical theory is far from being a statistical idea. Although we all agree that physics is a transformation of pure mathematics, since it takes into account a reality principle, no one would think of denying that the work of physicists is scientific. This is how physics and mathematics are related. But medicine's relation to mathematics is more distant, since the human sphere is not governed by the same laws as elements in the ordinary, "physical" world.

But psychiatry, a branch of medicine that Henri Ey called "a pathology of freedom", is even more distant from pure mathematics, because the psyche cannot be subjected to validations (EBM), which in medicine can be applied to certain specific pathophysiological conditions.

The fact is that medical science and particularly psychiatry have a specific nature, and that statistical reasoning can neither simply replace them nor give them easy scientific legitimacy. The human outlook involved is not suited to statistical reasoning. As Stephen Jay Gould reminds us: "Science is rooted in creative interpretation. Numbers suggest, constrain, and refute; they do not, by themselves, specify the content of scientific theories".[6] Therefore, we have everything to gain by continuing to defend the idea that the scope of medical science is much wider than the statistical perspective, and that although we can benefit from advances in that field, statistical validation must not be considered the only type of validation possible in medicine.

Indeed, C.S. Pierce,[7] in his methodical study of logical inferences, proposes three major types of signification: abduction, induction and deduction. Abduction submits a case to inference based on a rule and a result. Induction infers the rule from a particular case and its results. Deduction is the application of a general rule to a particular case.

While the last two significations are usually governed by classic scientific reasoning, the first – abduction – "is rooted in creative interpretation" and leads, most often thanks to the scientist's intuition and previous experience, to hypotheses to be tested later.[8] The immediate problem that arises is that abduction takes place in a particular epistemological space, while the two other forms of inference – and deduction even more than induction – tend towards generalisation and the risk of totalisation this facilitates.

But although totalisation and the multitude of deductions attached to it constitute the fantasy underlying a certain type of statistical research nowadays, we must remember that although this science, recent in the history of mathematics, is meant to help us with the speculative aspect of our work in psychiatry, it should serve to explore its opposite – particularisation. Nicolas Dodier, in a note on Alain Desrosières in *The Politics of Large Numbers,*[9] explores individual status in a world where statistics tend to generalise. Dodier reflects on:

> the condition of individuals when a partly autonomous statistical language is used. This question places ... in a new light the problem of the articulation. . . of statistical objects and concrete individuals. According to Desrosières, we now extend the epistemology of social sciences, usually focused on examining totalisation, to include the reverse operation, little-known but crucial: particularisation. The same question then arises outside the social sciences in fields like medicine . . . where individuals are subjected more and more often to the exigencies of statistical reasoning.[10]

There is no better way to describe the problem related to the abusive use of statistical reasoning in medicine:

> Once statistical reasoning has assembled all its tools, what will be its effects on concrete individuals? . . . Desrosières points out the fundamental antagonism – the incompatibility – between concern with the particular, seen in its diversity, and the erasure of this diversity by statistical reasoning.[11]

It does not seem acceptable for statisticians to exclude from their research the effects of their science on particular individuals. Under no circumstances can I consider statistical findings as objects to be transmitted by unscrupulous media directly to patients without the usual safeguards. Especially since the

> social sciences are faced with a characteristic of narrative discourse analysed in depth by [Paul] Ricoeur [in *Time and Narrative*]: all narrative is an act of configuration. . . . And this act of configuration strongly resists attempts at standardisation.[12]

In our practice, the best guarantor of these foundations is undoubtedly the psychotherapeutic process itself. In fact, the whole of the Freudian technique consists of a set of variations on prefiguration, figuration and configuration of the clinical material provided by the patient in the transference. This requires respecting the singularity of every patient . . . and each caregiver!

But respect for the individual requires that statistical reasoning be set aside. And "statistical reasoning evaluates the individual before the deed, while in configuration, he is evaluated after the deed, based on his narrative of it".[13] For instance, there is, on the one hand, the incidence of autism; and on the other hand, the autistic child brought to see me, with whom I enter into a therapeutic relation. But Dodier underscores another essential point: "A purely statistical activity is immoral by definition, for it is devoid of any notion of obligation to human beings".[14] I would add that such an activity is to be clearly distinguished from the ethics of prevention. We are faced with the fundamental problem of the immutable character of the two forms of reasoning, which is not to be confused with incompatibility. In the context of our discussion, the fact that statistics have become so prevalent in contemporary thinking can be said to be a means of defence through generalisation against individual psychic pain, a modern form of splitting and idealisation (Klein).

Let us take the example of a consultation in child psychiatry. When parents arrive with a binder full of statistics collected from the Internet, it is likely that anxiety about an as-yet-unexplained symptom in their child drove them to search for its cause. And rather than talking to their family doctor, they chose to ask the great contemporary Other, the Internet. Although this research does not offer any possibility for interpretation, at least they have the impression that the information can advance the work needed to help their child. And what information do they find? Mostly statistical data. But this data addresses all their concerns: if my child presents these signs, there is this degree of probability that he has this disease, and he therefore needs this treatment. Still, a certain worry remains, and the parents continue to ask themselves the only truly scientific and methodical question: "What if it's something else?" (Torrubia). And it is thanks to this insistence of their disquiet conscience and their parental ethics that they finally arrange to see a child psychiatrist. The meeting with the parents allows other aspects of the medical relation to play their role – aspects governed by a kind of wisdom which puts in perspective the different elements present in the child's history.

It is in this that a significant part of the child psychiatrist's talent lies: in bringing to light what the anguish of the family's psychic suffering attempts to cover over with statistical generalities.

But before looking at the effects of the statistical reasoning underlying the new international classifications in the DSM-5 which now "governs" psychiatric decisions, let us review Bleuler's discoveries.

Bleuler's Definition of Schizophrenia

Schizophrenia as defined by Bleuler is (still?) taught in medical schools.[15] Its semiology includes three major syndromes: dissociation, paranoid delusions and autism.

Dissociation

Dissociation designates a break in the psychic unity of a subject, leading to disorganisation in his mental activity. This internal process causes a loss of harmony between the different spheres of his psychic life (affect, thought, behaviour, language). Discordant senses of self are a clinical expression of dissociation.

Thought Disorders

Dissociation disrupts thought processes. Thinking loses coherence and logic and becomes disordered. The subject jumps from one idea to another with no logical transition; his word associations are incomprehensible.

Dissociation takes two significant forms: motor blocking and mental fatigue. Motor blocking manifests as a sudden halting of speech, or starting over on the same subject, or on a different subject. Mental fatigue hinders speech, which slows down and then goes back to its previous rhythm.

Speech Problems

The subject's speech does not seem intended to establish contact with an interlocutor. It contains neologisms, misuse of words (paralogisms), misuse of syntax (agrammatism), affected language (preciosity) and total or almost total lack of speech. Schizophrenia is associated with totally incoherent and incomprehensible language.

Changes in Reasoning

The schizophrenic subject has his own logic, which renders his speech bizarre and incomprehensible and his reasoning morbid. He displays alterations in his ability to reason.

Disorders of Affect Regulation

Affective discordance refers to affects that are not suited to the situation or to the thought expressed. The dissociation causes affective ambivalence. The schizophrenic subject is unable to deal with two contradictory feelings and choose between them. These affective disorders can lead to unforeseeable emotional behaviour.

Psychomotor Disorders

Psychomotor disorders observed in schizophrenia include unusual mannerisms, stereotypic movement (rocking, scratching . . .), echophenomena, echopraxia, negativism (refusal to shake the extended hand, shifty gaze . . .); in some cases, catalepsy: a loss of voluntary motion, fixed posture, "lead-pipe" rigidity.

Depersonalisation

Depersonalisation refers to a feeling of loss of psychic and physical integrity and of bodily disintegration, producing intense annihilation anxiety.

Paranoid Delusions

Paranoid delusions are disorganised. They are vague, incoherent, incomprehensible and chaotic. They take many forms (hallucinations, illusions, intuitions . . .) and have complicated themes (mystical delusions, persecution, conspiracy . . .). The subject's belief in his delusion is most often unshakable and can trigger behaviour problems (agitation, aggressivity, stupor . . .).

The Syndrome of Mental Automatism, strongly suggestive of schizophrenia, refers to the subject's loss of control over a portion of his thoughts. He perceives an echo of his thoughts, an insertion of commentary on his thoughts or actions. He has the impression that his thoughts are stolen or have been guessed, even manipulated.

Autism

Autism in schizophrenia[16] refers to a subject's altered relations to the world, characterised by loss of contact with reality (apragmatism, disinterest, emotional flatness, avolition, negligence . . .); withdrawal to inner life (phantasies, imaginary world, abstract and abstruse ideas . . .). The existence of this autistic universe causes severe social isolation.

Schizophrenia in the DSM-5

The definition given in the DSM-5[17] has been radically modified to make clinical signs correspond to hypothetical underlying mechanisms (cerebral and cognitive).

Positive Symptoms

These include changes in perceived experience, with disturbances in the subject's relation to the environment and to his own body (hallucinations, delusions). The hypothetical underlying mechanisms are increased subcortical dopamine synthesis, aberrant connectivity between the cortex and subcortical structures, trouble organising actions and social cognition disorders.

Negative Symptoms

The clinical description includes an inability to act and to experience or express emotions. The hypothetical underlying mechanisms listed are front hypodopaminergia, prefrontal cortical dysfunction, social cognition disorders and inhibited action initiation.

Disorganised Schizophrenia

Characteristic signs include disorganised behaviour and speech. The hypothetical underlying mechanisms are prefrontal cortex connectivity dysfunction and executive function disorder.

Neurocognitive Dysfunction

Poor learning and retention of verbal information, whether its source is internal or external, is a hallmark of cognitive impairment. The hypothetical underlying mechanisms are prefrontal cortex dysfunction, aberrant connectivity between the cortex and subcortical structures, as well as attention and memory deficit and executive function disorder.

Thus, the DSM-5 description is radically different in that it is based entirely on a neuroscientific hypothesis presented as probable, whose hoped-for validation, dating back to the DSM-IV (1994), seems to be evidence based on proof not yet obtained! Obviously, the rigorous standard of evidence-based medicine is not applied equally across the board.

Dissociated Transference: Jean Oury and the Primary Symptoms of Schizophrenia

At Ginette Michaud's invitation, Jean Oury gave twelve lectures at the Institute of Psychology, Paris Diderot University, between November 1984 and May 1986. They were published in *Les symptoms primaires de la schizophrénie*[18] (The Primary Symptoms of Schizophrenia). This book is a treasure of intelligence and humanity, outlining Bleuler's discoveries and providing a synthesis of Oury's perspective on the care of schizophrenic patients. Today, this book helps us to maintain an ethical position in the arduous fight to defend a humane form of psychiatry. In it, Oury also provides numerous clues shedding light on the complex factors involved in this form of psychiatric practice, in a context which, as we all know, is undermined by constant and outrageous simplification of human problems.

Following in the footsteps of his friend and master Tosquelles, Oury embodies the renewal of psychoanalysis, provided its practice is extended to the field of severe psychopathologies such as schizophrenia and archaic pathologies in general. But in order to arrive at these innovations, Oury had to reconsider the entire sphere of psychiatry. He combines his original concepts with bibliographical knowledge and refers widely to the arts, literature, the sciences and history; this renders his teaching vibrant and depicts psychiatry with a humane face. Although psychoanalysis plays a central role in this psychiatric model, Oury always avoided the temptation to turn it into a fetish. He was opposed to attempts to separate psychiatry from psychoanalysis; not that they merged together in his thinking, but rather that he considered them to be irreducibly linked by the ethical pact governing practice. In his university lectures, Oury presented many historical, philosophical, medical, scientific, anthropological and political facts concerning the schizophrenias in order to compose a complex narrative. This narrative included biological and genetic aspects, as well as more psychopathological, contextual, phenomenological and institutional aspects. In short, Oury presented his research, revealing the complexity of the subject.

I feel it is important for our discussion to underscore certain aspects of Oury's endeavour. First, the form taken by this endeavour – twelve lectures given at the university on the primary symptoms of schizophrenia – exceeded by far the primary symptoms announced in advance.

In fact, it was as if Oury had decided to assess the situation in the middle of his voyage on the Ocean of Madness, to let us know what conclusions he had drawn thus far. But aside from this assessment of the situation, he also made it clear, as early as 1984–1986, that he was angry with "despisers" of a certain traditional psychiatry. He saw the progression towards the DSM-III of that era, reinforced since then by the successive publication of the DSM-IV and DSM-5, as a serious regression in the treatment of schizophrenic patients, making it possible to reduce contemporary psychiatry to the "veterinary psychiatry" denounced by Georges Daumezon in his era. Searching for pathognomonic signs is not new, and rather than restricting it to biological signs, the search should be extended to all possible manifestations of schizophrenia, including, as Oury points out in his book, infralinguistic spheres such as the "pathic moment" (Erwin Straus). Now that the (available) letters exchanged between Freud and Bleuler have been published, it is interesting to see that this debate was already causing violent clashes at the time between the sides represented by Kraepelin and Bleuler. In fact, the classification proposed by the former at the end of the 19th century and used until the beginning of the 20th century aimed to settle the essential question of diagnosing dementia praecox. Kraepelin describes the signs of the disease accurately, but he is attentive, above all, to the types of deterioration seen in the patient as the disease progresses. The designation "dementia praecox" strongly emphasises the losses suffered by the patient at the cognitive, affective and behavioural levels.

According to Bleuler, dementia praecox is a screen behind which one must look for the person of the schizophrenic.[19] And we must not lose sight of the fact that Bleuler, who already admired Freud for his work on aphasias (1891), would become one of his close collaborators during a crucial period in the development of psychoanalysis – the period between 1904 and 1913 – partly through his connection to Carl Jung. Relations between Freud and Bleuler remained cordial practically until Freud's death, as shown by the last letters they exchanged. Bleuler questioned Freud about transference in schizophrenia. For Freud, his encounter with Bleuler was important for several reasons, some of which we will discuss as the most relevant to our topic.

Freud did not venture very far into the sphere of the psychoses; constrained to set up private practice because his university career was blocked given his Jewish origins, he came into contact with neurotic patients. Yet, despite his lack of spontaneous interest in these pathologies, he never lost his intellectual interest in this major psychiatric question. In fact, he authored some remarkable contributions to the subject, including the famous monograph based on President Schreber's autobiographical work. Freud, whose position vis-à-vis the University of Vienna was tenuous, knew that the topic of the psychoses was fundamental if his invention of psychoanalysis was to gain access to the world of medicine and psychiatry. Bleuler, a recognised academic, who intimated to Freud that his research had become one of the pillars of university teaching in Zurich, was going to provide this opportunity. It was in this context that Bleuler and Freud started a correspondence about major psychoanalytic concepts, particularly transference in psychosis, and their possible "usefulness" in the understanding of these serious pathologies. It is interesting to note that the term "dissociation", which designates the primary symptoms of schizophrenia, offers a counterpoint to the term "free association", which guides the psychoanalytic method in the treatment. Being able or unable to associate is a crucial idea for a better comprehension of Oury's emphasis on the concept of "dissociated transference", and Tosquelles's insistence on "multireferential transference". The new name given to dementia praecox – schizophrenia – and the developments that followed, are thus very closely linked with the work done by Bleuler with Freud and Jung on the manner in which a patient undergoing a primary process – dissociation – defends himself by developing secondary symptoms such as paranoid delusions which, in this context, constitute an attempt at self-healing. When viewing these events from a historical perspective, we might ask ourselves if the cooling of relations between the two men, aside from specific difficulties concerning Jung, was not caused in part by divergent views on their experiences with the transferential relation, which were substantially different given the patients concerned: neurotic in Freud's case and schizophrenic in Bleuler's.

While the standard psychoanalytic method is suited to treating the first type of patient, it is vastly insufficient for treating the second. At Burghölzli in Zurich, Bleuler made a courageous attempt at using psychoanalysis, but the difficulties that arose in the transferential process caused him to forgo his close ties with Freud and with psychoanalysis, and to resign from the International Psychoanalytic Association.

However, a colleague of Bleuler's and a student of Auguste Forel who had emigrated to the United States, Adolph Meyer, was interested in Freud, whom he met on the occasion of the Clark University Lectures, given by Freud with Jung and Ferenczi. Meyer played an important role in promoting the expansion of psychoanalysis in America; he believed it to offer great hope for the mentally ill and was certain of the rapid success of its implementation. Indeed, Meyer saw schizophrenia as a highly reactive psychosis and concluded that patients would be amenable to psychotherapy. Harry Stack Sullivan[20] also developed a body of concepts on this subject, deeply influencing American psychiatry. These teachings gave rise to the concept of "schizophrenic reaction/reactive schizophrenia", which Jean Oury discussed on numerous occasions.

Elsewhere in Europe, Kurt Schneider, Karl Jasper's pupil and a psychiatrist and philosopher influenced for a time by Bleuler's hypotheses, chose to return to Kraepelin's perspective when describing the major symptoms of schizophrenia. His work, introduced in the United States by William Mayer-Gross, would become the foundation of the future international classification of the DSM-III (1980). Although the first classifications had still been strongly influenced by psychoanalysis, starting with the DSM-III, when Kurt Schneider's concepts emerged and profoundly altered the referential basis of classifications, especially given that neuroleptics, invented in the 1950s and prescribed starting in 1953–54, radically changed psychiatric reasoning, reinforcing the idea – or rather the phantasy – that hard biological science can provide the answer in terms of treatment and ascertain the medico-mimetic etiology of mental disorders.

Taking a totally different perspective, Oury cuts across different theoretical currents and proposes a model of psychiatry which brings together these various discoveries without opposing them, to let them exert complementary effects and in so doing contribute to improving the lives of the mentally ill, particularly schizophrenics. He cites the example of his friend Roland Kühn, psychiatrist and psychoanalyst who was Binswanger's successor at Munterlinden and an avid reader of Freud's complete works, as well as an eminent phenomenologist and a prescribing psychiatrist who discovered imipramine in 1957 when he observed the unexpected antidepressant effects of a supposed experimental neuroleptic.

In Jean Oury's view, the schizophrenic suffers from disorders which, despite and beyond their visible primary symptoms, are essentially rhythm disorders (Maldiney), disorders of "bodily presence" (Jürg Zutt), of emergence (Oury); disruptions of taking shape, of incarnation (Pankow), of semblance (Lacan); in short, disorders that subject the patient to a degree of archaic anguish incompatible with the life of a "normosed" individual (Jean Ayme). Oury suggests calling the site of the hellish experience of the schizophrenic a "point of horror", located behind a mirror that does not bring together the fragments of a scattered body, dissociated, under the benevolent gaze of the parent, the one who holds responsibility for the other (Levinas).

In order to improve the life of the schizophrenic, Jean Oury conceived a type of environment in total contrast with the point of horror, calling it a "point of dawn", constituted of possible spaces of precarious coalescence of the body image, spaces in which pathic features and "ambiance" are present in daily life strongly enough to resist entropy by relying on the impulse for anarchy[21] always at work in these borderline pathologies.

The particularity of the institution is that is makes possible the potential containment of dissociated transferences, thanks to the professionals who live with the schizophrenic patients. This is what gave the invention of institutional psychotherapy its value: the fact that it produced both a theoretical justification and concrete results. The "transferential constellation" is one of these results.

As part of his work, Oury, in collaboration with others,[22] was able to establish the La Borde Clinic and to make possible many local institutional psychotherapeutic projects. In addition, he was able to teach us the practice in unconventional ways by exposing us to his commitment to transference and its numerous harmonic resonances, which allowed him to develop a theory and ensuing practice worthy of the name.

Consequently, his teaching is an essential work tool, since instead of simply proposing a protocol to be applied, Oury confronts us to our own practices and ideas, asking us to invent the rest, taking into account our patients, our history, our context, our friends. This teaching will no doubt continue to resonate in our minds for a long time, perpetuating its rich ramifications.

Notes

1 Bleuler, E., *Dementia Praecox or the Group of Schizophrenias*, Madison, CT, USA: International Universities Press, 1968.
2 Bleuler, E., *The Prognosis of Dementia Praecox: Group of Schizophrenias*, available at www.lacanianWorksExchange.net
3 Bleuler, E., *Dementia Praecox or the Group of Schizophrenias*, op. cit.
4 Bottéro, A., "Une Histoire de la dissociation schizophrénique", *L'Évolution Psychiatrique* 66, 2001, p. 56.
5 The weather forecast should tell us something about the reliability of statistical data.
6 Gould, S.J., *The Mismeasure of Man*, New York: W.W. Norton, 1983.
7 Delion, P., *L'enfant autiste, le bébé et la sémiotique*, Paris: PUF, 2000.
8 Laffitte, P.J., *Le langage en deçà des mots*, Paris: Éditions d'une, 2021.
9 Desrosières, A., *The Politics of Large Numbers*, Cambridge, MA: Harvard University Press, 2002.
10 Dodier, N., "Les sciences sociales face à la raison statistique" (criticalreview), *Annales, Histoire, Sciences Sociales*, no. 2, 1996, pp. 409–428.
11 Ibid., p. 417.
12 Ibid., p. 420.
13 Ibid., p. 424.
14 Ibid., p. 425.
15 www-sante.ujf-grenoble.fr/SANTE/1/7.
16 In a 1943, Leo Kanner admitted borrowing the term "autism" from Bleuler. But when he added "infantile" to this term, he described a developmental pathology that has little to do with autism in schizophrenia, except withdrawal into oneself, away from the world.
17 Frank, N., "Childhood onset schizophrenia", *Archives de Pédiatrie* 20, 2013, pp. 789–799.
18 Oury, J., *Les symptômes primaires de la schizophrénie*, Paris: Éditions d'une, 2016.
19 Wyrsch, J., *La personne du schizophrène. Étude clinique, psychologique, anthropophénoménologique*, Paris: PUF, 1956.
20 Sullivan, H.S., *Schizophrenia as a Human Process*, New York: Norton & Company, 1974.
21 Zaltzman, N., *De la guérison psychanalytique*, Paris: PUF, 1994.
22 Roulot, D., *Schizophrénie et langage. Que veut dire le mot « chapeau »*? Toulouse: érès, 2004; Lecarpentier, M., "Logique existentielle, transfert et management de l'accompagnement", *Empan*, no. 110, 2018.

Chapter 4

Adhesive and Projective Transference in Children

Children do not exist without parents. The forms of transference specific to them are reflections of these unavoidable intersubjective relations. They are at the origin of everything that ensues. Contrary to the continuous misinformation streaming on certain social media sites and claiming that psychoanalysts blame the parents, this parent/child alliance is fundamental to any psychotherapeutic work with a child, especially when the latter suffers from an archaic pathology. A child can progress if his parents accompany him in this evolution.

While the concept of dissociated transference is suitable in schizophrenia, it is useful to examine more closely what is at play where children with archaic disorders are concerned. Whether those in favor of international classifications like it or not, for my discussion I must distinguish between forms of autism and infantile psychoses.

History of the Notion of Infantile Psychosis

This concept is indispensable to clinicians who work with its manifestations in their daily practice. It is interesting to note that the word "psychosis"[1], so crucial in the history of psychiatry, gave rise to countless arguments when it came to describing the clinical reality pertaining to children displaying signs strangely similar to those seen in adults diagnosed with psychosis. I shall not dwell on the different propositions at the heart of quarrels between competing currents as widely opposed as those opting for very early-onset dementia and those preferring to speak of infantile schizophrenia. In the end, the term *infantile psychosis* won out. Roger Misès, a passionate proponent of the term, insisted on the specificity of clinical signs in children as compared to those seen in adults. The particularity of this nosographic category applying to children – in other words, to developing beings – even made him specify that in some cases

DOI: 10.4324/9781003380269-4

the young patient could become "trapped" in the web of a pathology that constitutes a disorganizing element for his development, such as severe epilepsy, for example, or any other diagnosed physical illness that could modify the developmental process.

Many clinicians still remember the success encountered by the term "evolutive disharmony of a psychotic nature". This term distinguished between adult psychoses as stabilised processes, and the radically different nature of disorders in developing children. But Misès, who was also interested in autism, insisted with his usual thoroughness that these disorders were the earliest forms of infantile psychoses. At that time, the main objective of the so-called French classification of mental disorders in children and adolescents, later expanded to include babies, was to link nosographic descriptions with psychopathology and, more importantly, to treatment recommendations.

But, for reasons historians will one day help us to elucidate, the word "psychosis" continues to be associated with the psychiatrist and, consequently, with *madness*, so that all those affected by the latter have to seek the help of the former. By contrast, the latest scientific discoveries in the field of genetics encouraged those seduced by a simplified explanation of the human, planting in their minds the idea that autism has nothing to do with psychosis, since its etiology would soon be explained by hard science, making it *de facto* a physical illness whose relational and epigenetic aspects are negligible. At last, the management of these children would be entrusted to experts in genetics and neurodevelopment. There would be no more need for psychiatrists and no more connotation of madness. There would be no more talk of psychosis, a concept seen as the sign of contamination by obsolete theories, starting with psychoanalysis – judging by the hardships the latter would suffer. You had only to pursue psychoanalytic training, use psychoanalytic concepts, give lectures and/or write articles containing a reference to psychoanalytic psychopathology, and you were placed in a category of individuals with whom it was inappropriate to communicate, to exchange, to do research, to publish, and whose ideas, opinions and practices were untrustworthy. If you "compromised yourself" with psychoanalysis, you could no longer treat autistic children and had to limit yourself to treating the others – those who are not autistic – the psychotic ones. But if you look for them in the international classifications, these children don't exist either: they have simply been eliminated from the DSM-IV and DSM-5 for complex reasons.[2]

But what happened to these children Misès described so frequently? Not to worry: they were included in the category "Pervasive disorder not otherwise specified". Following the "enhancements" made to the DSM-5, they are found under "autism spectrum disorder".

Treating Archaic Pathologies in Children

The forms of autism classified under the general category "autism spectrum disorder" are the ones which primarily constitute archaic pathologies in children. But we shall attempt to show that they are not the only ones.

Autism

Leo Kanner considered infantile autism to have two major symptoms: aloneness and sameness – that is, the aloneness inherent to autism and the requirement for an unmodified physical environment. He also pointed to speech difficulties (late language acquisition and use) and psychomotor difficulties (stereotyped movements and difficulty establishing relations with others, even at the preverbal level). Since autism was first described in 1943, numerous studies have pointed out complementary signs, have proposed associating autism with other major syndromes (infantile psychoses) and have recently extended the list of manifestations covered by the term (in the DSM-5).

*Diagnostic Criteria for Autism Spectrum Disorder
in the DSM-5*

"**A**   Persistent deficits in social communication and social interaction:

1   Deficits in socio-emotional reciprocity.
2   Deficits in nonverbal communicative behaviors.
3   Deficits in developing, maintaining and understanding relationships.

B   Restricted, repetitive patterns of behavior, interests or activities.

1   Stereotyped or repetitive motor movements, use of objects or speech.
2   Insistence on sameness, inflexible adherence to routines or ritualized patterns of verbal or nonverbal behavior.
3   Highly restricted, fixated interests that are abnormal in intensity or focus.
4   Hyper or hypo reactivity to sensory input or unusual interest in sensory aspects of the environment.

C   Symptoms must be present in the early development period.
D   Symptoms cause clinically significant impairment in social, occupa-
    tional or other important areas of current functioning.
E   These disturbances are not better explained by intellectual disability
    . . . or global developmental delay".

Although this new description compiles the signs observed in the
entire field of the autism spectrum, it leaves out children with another
form of archaic pathology which does not fit this general description of
autism spectrum disorders.

INFANTILE PSYCHOSES

Indeed, we regularly see children brought for psychiatric consultation[3] for
whom we recommend psychiatric treatment, who present signs of psychic
suffering which do not correspond to the description of infantile autism.
Often, their development is normal until the age of 18 months to 2 years.
The behavioural problems they display are "excessive", as opposed to
the "insufficient" types of behaviour seen in autistic children (deficits in
communication and ability to relate, withdrawal). Psychotic children are
intrusive with people around them; they keep wanting to "run into them"
(Geneviève Haag), contrary to autistic children who remain "stuck" to
an object or a person. Psychotic children are always looking around to
meet a gaze that will confirm a threat of persecution, and their behaviour always seems to be determined by a basic assumption[4] of fight-
flight which governs their action despite themselves. Their language
skills, often advanced, become a defensive weapon wielded forcefully
and brutally, rather than being a communication tool serving to solve a
certain problem. Their family often observes them to be fundamentally
aggressive, and sees their aggression turn to violence even at a very
young age. In most cases, this is to be seen as an inappropriate defensive
reaction of the psychotic child against attempts by parents and siblings at
making contact with him.
    Although problematic behaviours can be handled by the child's
family in the first three years – through adjustments that sometimes
adversely affect the other children in the family – the illness can no
longer be ignored when the child starts to go to school. From the start,
the teacher informs the parents that their child's behaviour is incompatible with being in a classroom unless special support is provided
and urges them to consult an expert in developmental problems as
soon as possible.

The parents often react by admitting the painful reality of the problems they have been facing with the child in their own home and they start to look for a child psychiatrist who can give them a diagnosis to explain the child's condition and can start to treat him with his team of specialists. But sometimes the parents' reaction is denial, refutation of the teacher's observations or a need to blame the teacher. In that case, the child's journey will be chaotic, he will meet with rejection at school and will be rejected by other children, until circumstances force the parents, sometimes after considerable time, to acknowledge their child's illness and provide him with the help he needs.

International classifications no longer describe this illness in a "positive" manner, as a means of making a medical diagnosis, identifying the infantile psychosis process at work, and recommending treatment to limit the major developmental disorders that inevitably appear. This type of illness is only designated by elimination and is included with forms of autism despite the fact that the classic signs of the latter are absent. It is as if infantile psychosis was a poor relative of autism, a sort of relic that puts a strain on the splendid modern edifice built for "Autism". Autism has become the gold standard of child psychiatry practice. Moreover, statistically, the number of autistic children is much smaller than that of children with PDD/ASD who are not autistic, many of whom are psychotic.

Understanding Forms of Transference Specific to Archaic Childhood Pathologies

All this is very unfortunate, because if a diagnosis of infantile psychosis is made by elimination, treatment recommendations will also follow this indirect reasoning, and the treatment strategy will be elaborated on the same imperialistic basis.

Indeed, treatment of children with these infantile psychotic disorders and other developmental disharmonies characteristic of psychotic structure is not comparable to therapy suitable for autistic children. It's not that they might not benefit from the three-faceted management I recommend for all PDD/ASD children: educational always, pedagogical if possible, and therapeutic if necessary; but the psychopathological mechanisms governing their "being-in-the-world" are different. In autistic children, the internal world is governed by psychic processes founded on pathological "adhesive identification", while in psychotic children these psychic processes stem from pathological "projective identification".

This confirms extensive research that has been conducted for a long time, particularly by Kleinian and post-Kleinian psychoanalysts who were able to approach most closely the internal worlds of these children, allowing us to understand their psychopathological mechanisms and, as a result, to design helpful therapies for them.

The psychiatry suited to these specific therapies integrates the various constructive aspects of medicine in general, including the latest scientific advances as well as the quality of the doctor/patient relationship and the patient's environment, that is, the conditions of daily life in the family.

In a context of infantile psychosis, it is important to take into account the specific mechanisms governing the "being-in-the-world" of these children in order to adapt to the particularity of their transference, which I propose to call "projective transference". It is useful to distinguish two major types of transference with children presenting severe pathologies such as autism and psychosis.

The transference characterizing autistic children is "adhesive transference". It is largely based on the observable fact that these children build their world with the aforementioned mechanisms of adhesive identification, normal at first and later pathological. These psychic processes are a partial answer to their almost constant need to cope with the most primitive archaic anxieties. It is easy to understand that pathological adhesive identity shaped by archaic clinging reflexes – which prompted John Bowlby to develop attachment theory as a necessary adjunct to psychoanalytic theory – would be very useful in these circumstances. If I fall from a cliff, I cling to anything that can offer support. If each time I cross a threshold this anxiety seizes me, I cling to anything I can get hold of, even to myself. To cling to oneself is the most extreme expression of autism. By contrast, the psychoses are more complex because they emerge at later stages of development, often after some language acquisition. These children experience less disorganizing archaic anxiety – not necessarily less severe – than autistic children.

These anxieties observed in autistic children correspond to the "primitive agony" described by Winnicott in his paper on fear of breakdown, and specifically to the most primitive: "falling forever". When you see these children day after day, it is relatively easy to understand what happens. Each time such an anxiety is felt, the child clings to you, his body grabbing on to your body; you will carry the indelible traces of his grip on your body in the form of various scars on the back of your hands, on your forearms, around your neck. These injuries testify to the moments when you were the life-saving support of the child tormented by his primitive anxieties. I propose designating these transferential mementos as "adhesiles", embodied signs of the specific character of adhesive transference. From a certain perspective, these are "formations of the unconscious" (Lacan) of the child, who constructs himself in the transference with one or several caregivers; these formations reflect the level of his anxieties and of the defenses he sets in place to protect himself from them in order to survive in a hostile archaic milieu.

As for psychotic children, their formations of the unconscious are often intrusive, invasive, even violent. But as they develop, they find other means – of a more psychic nature – to manifest themselves in and through the transference: you wake up from a nightmare in which the psychotic child persecutes you, your thoughts dwell on him when you are not in direct contact with him, you have vivid and sometimes persecutory fantasies about him. The child was able to use his projective identification mechanisms to fight his own persecutory anxiety states, and thus "attack and flee" to take refuge in your psychic apparatus, where he feels protected and contained, at the cost of a certain psychic suffering inflicted on his therapists. I suggest calling the weapons he uses in transference "projectiles", closely related to what Bion called "bizarre objects" in search of a "thought-thinking apparatus" that they never encounter. The art of the therapist consists of placing his psychic apparatus at the disposal of psychotic children without exceeding the "maximum permissible dose" of projectiles to transform, so as to avoid burnout.

This is a far cry from the simplistic 2012 recommendations of the French National Authority for Health, recommendations that have been met with defiance by child psychiatrists and even by the highly respected journal *Prescrire*[5] which pointed out in the clearest terms significant discrepancies in the Authority's scientific claims.

Now that we have laid these premises, let us see how the transferential constellation can help to create a place for, and treat, archaic pathologies.

Notes

1 Ernst von Feuchtersleben used this term to describe mental illness in 1845 in his *Psychology Manual*. The term was used in "in a general sense, to mean an illness of the mind, as opposed to neuroses, which designated nervous disorders without detectable lesions, in which mental disturbances were considered unstable" (Pastel, J., Quétel, C., *Nouvelle histoire de la psychiatrie*, Paris: Privat, 1983, p. 627.

2 I direct the reader to Michel Minard's excellent work *Le DSM roi*, érès, 2013.

3 Delion, P., *La consultation avec l'enfant*, Paris: Masson, 2010.

4 In his book *Experiences in Groups and Other Papers* (Routledge, 1968), Bion describes how each group's conscious aims are determined by three types of unconscious basic assumptions: dependence, pairing and fight-flight.

5 *Prescrire*, vol. 33, no. 352, 2013, p. 305.

Chapter 5

The Transferential Constellation

"Constellation" is a word normally reserved for speaking about the stars. A group of stars can be a valuable compass for navigators lost on the open sea. Thus, there was every reason for the transferential constellation to become a valuable means of guiding patients lost on the sea of madness.

Defined as the totality of caregivers in contact with the patient presenting an archaic pathology, the constellation is the result of long-term collective work carried out by the team treating that patient. All the members of the institutional team should feel involved in the transferential constellation. It is not a matter of choosing the caregivers to be included in the constellation and excluding others, but rather for everyone present to ask: "Who is in contact with this patient?" Next, everyone has to agree to meet with all concerned. Sometimes it is helpful to bring other elements into this transferential constellation of human beings, such as animals or objects that are particularly important to the patient. Moreover, the transferential constellation can exist in all contexts of psychiatric care, whether the patient is hospitalised or not, without it affecting the treatment mode chosen by caregivers.

The quality of the contact between the patient and the people involved with him is very variable. With some, contact is frequent, prolonged and supportive, while with others it is sporadic, persecutory and tangential. The important thing is to maintain contact. The notion of contact has been the object of remarkable research conducted by Léopold Szondi and Jacques Schotte. In Schotte's anthropopsychiatry,[1] ensuing from a long and fruitful collaboration with Szondi[2] – inventor of depth psychology – the contact vector[3] holds an important place. In his view of psychopathology, Schotte borrows the Szondian categories of "contact", "sexual", "paroxysmal" and "schizomorph", proposing a double reading – ontological and ontic – in which Freudian theories are abundantly

DOI: 10.4324/9781003380269-5

illustrated, since Schotte's hypothesis states that the different psychiatric disorders are forms of decompensation in structures already bearing their own line of cleavage (the crystal metaphor proposed by Freud in 1914), and that each human being has the potential of presenting all the forms of decompensation.

In this psychopathology, the first dimensions, related to contact, concern moods, manic-depressive decompensation and all dependent personality disorders. This dimension is particularly important because the contact precedes the object, confirming one of the main ideas related to preobjectal transference in archaic disorders.

At the root of this question of contact, to which Szondi gave a central place in his fate analytic system, there are several years of dialogue between Leopold Szondi and Imre Hermann. Szondi borrowed from the latter the concepts designating the different instinctual forms of contact: for example, "to cling" and "to take hold", based on Hermann's terms. What Hermann intended, based both on his clinical experience and comparative ethology, was to examine the origins of Freudian instincts, prior to the developments of the notion of erotisation at which Freud stopped.[4]

To paraphrase Jean Mélon, Schotte's formulations: send for, come, go, send off, are much more pertinent because by emphasising the back-and-forth they bring attention to the question of rhythm at the origin of the primordial structuration of space and time, regardless of their reference to any object, of their conventional organisation and of their acquisition by a subject whose life will come to an end.[5]

The notion of "contact vector" is similar to Charles S. Pierce's "firstness"[6] and to Erwin Straus' concept of a "pathic"[7] mode of sensing. For Pierce, firstness, secondness and thirdness constitute the basic triad of semiotics. The second element of the triad is the sign – or "representation" in Michel Balat's language - with its object and its interpretant.

For Pierce, "firstness is a characteristic the mode of which consists in its subject's being positively such as it is regardless of anything else. This is simply a . . . possibility".[8] Gérard Deledalle elucidates further:

> The idea of the absolutely first must be entirely separated from all conception of or reference to anything else. . . . The first must therefore be present and immediate, so as not to be second to a representation. . . . The first is that whose being is simply in itself, not referring to anything.[9]

Deledalle reminds the reader that for Pierce "firstness consists in the subject's being such as it is regardless of anything else".[10] In his book

Regard, parole, espace, Henri Maldiney[11] introduces the concept of the "pathic", created by Erwin Straus. Maldiney considers the pathic to be a dimension of affectivity allowing us to communicate with the material world (hyletic data), without any reference to a particular perceived object. "If we linked the pathic moment with objects, we would be reintroducing it into the field of the conceptual, and the distinction between the gnostic and pathic would be already annulled". But here another reasoning applies, and "this reasoning is an aesthetic that can be fully expressed in terms of time and space. This is Straus' phenomenological approach to sensing and behaviour, his phenomenology of time and space".[12]

This quote makes it possible to show that the dimensions of the pathic, of firstness and of contact are at the heart of what is at stake in the archaic, and subsequently in the conditions necessary for being receptive to and working with these forms of transference.

Taken together, they can help us understand primitive identification phenomena such as *adhesive* and *projective identification*. The notion of contact points to an initial dimension of transference in the encounter with another. This will be the foundation on which other dimensions will be built, to complete a common human experience. Each caregiver in contact with the patient will constitute a point of refuge for the patient, and a container for his (bodily-) psychic elements in the transference. Based on these encounters, the caregiver will gradually create (and work through) a narrative of what he feels, what he goes through, what he experiences in regard to the patient. But the individual position does not always make it possible to construct such a narrative.

In this respect, the transferential constellation provides a necessary group dimension: I will be able to tell the story of the experiences I had with this patient to my colleagues in the constellation. By doing this, thoughts, which could be imprecise, vague, diffuse, incomplete or even repressed, will be woven into a narrative that defines my position as the witness to what I experienced with this patient, in view of what the others experienced. This is where particularities emerge, depending on the experiences of different caregivers with the same patient. The transferential constellation makes this possible but, above all, it invites each caregiver to tell his story honestly, while accepting the reality of the stories of the other caregivers, even when they are different or opposed to his own.

I see this second characteristic as an essential role of the transferential constellation. Indeed, a certain caregiver can be seen by the patient as the good object – to use Melanie Klein's term – in Tosquelles' story the janitor and the nurse played this role, while the psychiatrist was the bad object. It is not at all a matter of establishing who is right, or worse, deciding who the good object is, in order to ignore or exclude the bad object. Good and bad Kleinian objects are partial objects. In a context of archaic pathologies, it is essential that the qualities attributed to partial objects be taken together so as to overcome dissociation, splitting and all the psychopathological mechanisms associated with these preobjectal disorders. Indeed, the patient cannot resolve such an aporia on his own. The therapeutic function of the transferential constellation consists of allowing him to recognise in the figures of the caregivers elements of himself, good and bad, which he is unable to "integrate" by means of his own psychic strength. As a result, he can benefit from a containing function which makes him whole, enabling him – if only for a moment – to experience this unstabilised wholeness, that he is lacking, in institutional corporal-psychic envelopes – the transferential constellation.

A patient with an archaic pathology is entrusted to a team to be treated. The phoric (carrying) function of the team, which qualifies it to work with the patient, is the main therapeutic function to keep in mind collectively as the work begins. From that point on, the caregivers have different experiences with the patient, becoming consciously and unconsciously the "carriers" of these transferential elements. They also perform a semaphoric function which consists of carrying the enigmatic signs of the story of the patient's illness. In most cases, one caregiver alone cannot interpret what the patient transmits to him (his counter-transference); he needs to share these transferential elements with his colleagues. The meeting of the transferential constellation opens into a third logical stage, the metaphoric function, which makes it possible to connect each caregiver's narrative with those of the others, as they are presented in their original and productive heterogeneity, leading, in some instances, to the comprehension of the patient's signs, to a meaning hitherto hidden from the patient himself and from the caregivers. After the transferential constellation meeting, what is needed is not futile attempts at interpretation carried out with the patient, but rather to arrive naturally at an attitude towards him that results from what has been understood of his personal story. Jean Ayme called this the "interpretive attitude".[13] It is clear that the transferential constellation is the motor of the institutional "reactor".

But what are the conditions needed for it to produce expected results?

Institutional Effects . . .

On Archaic Pathologies

The quality of the transferential constellation device depends on that of the meeting which gives it concrete form in the institutional reality. Indeed, another particularity of dissociated transference and of *adhesiles* and *projectiles* is that they are deployed beneath the surface of ordinary object relations (neurotic), forcing us to consider the institution which treats these children or adults as a coordinated whole, rather than merely a team composed of parts disconnected from each other. The current tendency to consider caregivers interchangeable makes no sense. Given that it is to the team of caregivers that adhesive and projective dissociated transferences are addressed, the device making it possible to think them through is the transferential constellation meeting; that is, the time space in which members of the team in contact with a patient can really talk about their specific countertransference, without adopting the usual reasoning seen in groups, called "group mentality" (Bion): "Oh, this child needs some firm discipline rather than all this hyperspecialised care!" – with all the members of the team agreeing. This is how group mentality works. But in other teams, when one member says: "If this continues, this patient will drive me crazy!", another member might say that "he would be very happy to accompany this patient on a therapeutic outing". The possibility of expressing different opinions without being subjected to the *unifying* pressure of the group is a sign of good institutional health. As we can see, certain conditions must exist for transferential constellation meetings to be held; one important condition is the assurance that each person's account of his countertransference be respected as such, that each person's account will have the same value as those of the others, so that the transformation produced may have "containing" effects on the patient discussed.

In the case of Morgan, an autistic child treated at the day hospital, who does not keep his appointments with his child psychiatrist, his speech therapist, his psychomotor therapist or his special-needs teacher, but spends his time clinging to Janine, the hospital services worker whose job is to improve the children's meals, the team has a choice between two strategic therapeutic options: it can either consider that the meeting concerns professionals with official qualifications, and the clinical discussion will be relatively limited and will produce few ideas pertinent to active treatment, or it can take note of the fact that Morgan has an almost exclusive relationship with Janine, invite her to the meeting and, based on the clinical fact of this relationship, create a treatment that takes into account this adhesive transference, enabling the introduction of a psychotherapeutic perspective. Does this mean that Janine can go into private practice as a psychotherapist? This is not what she would want. But her participation in the transferential constellation as the first link in the treatment is crucial for Morgan.

Several factors determine the choice that will be made.

First, the usual hierarchical mode of functioning of a team is decisive in the process. If it is a corporate, vertical mode, the decisions of the leader will be applied imperatively, in the etymological sense (by order of the emperor), so that the people carrying out the decision have nothing to say about it; only the leader's decision determines crucial outcomes. This statutory hierarchy is necessary in certain situations. But in our psychiatric field, although we can accept this rule-based reasoning because each of us is hired as a psychiatrist, psychologist or nurse, and receives a salary based on that status, for reasons related to the transference we are not limited to this approach alone. It can sometimes be necessary, but it is insufficient. We must expand it by adding another hierarchy, one that is "subjectal" and results from transferential reasoning.

The transferential constellation as we have defined it brings together the people in contact with a patient. It is hard to imagine that a psychiatrist would tell a member of the constellation to follow a protocol established in advance in his relationship with the patient. By contrast, in the transferential mode of functioning, the possibility of speaking *a posteriori* about the experience shared with the patient is absolutely necessary for gaining a better grasp on the patient's clinical reality and its underlying mechanisms, and as a result, elaborate a better response to the archaic anxieties he too often endures alone. In addition, we have known for some time that these archaic disorders frequently cause institutional disputes, embroiling the treatment team in harmful conflicts, if they are not sufficiently analyzed and linked as closely as need be to the pathologies treated. This came to light as a result of the famous study conducted by Stanton and Schwartz at Chestnut Lodge in the United States and made known in France by Paul-Claude Racamier in his seminal work *Le psychanalyste sans divan* (The Psychoanalyst without a Couch).[14] Several therapists work with a schizophrenic patient who projects onto each of them elements that sometimes oppose each other, produced by the dissociation process to which he is subjected. This may cause hostile relations to develop due to the dissociated quality of the transference developed with each caregiver – a situation which greatly complicates the task of the treatment team, which has become the site of the hostilities playing out in the dissociated internal world of the schizophrenic, projected onto several members of the team, who are confused by the emotions deposited in them, often without realizing it clearly. Stanton and Schwartz conclude that it is crucial to hold regular meeting to speak freely about the conflicts that come to light, in order to transform them. They also observe that the sum of countertransferences experienced by the members of the transferential constellation have an anti-dissociative effect which transforms elements projected separately into complementary elements coming from the same person. This translates into a containing function, and even a protective shield which has almost immediate effects on the patient involved. Oury,[15] who extended Stanton and Schwartz's principle during his lengthy experience with dissociated transference, showed us how to place the transferential constellation in the service of adhesive and projective types of transference, seen particularly in children with archaic disorders.

Finally, these meetings make it possible to present to parents and associates, without breaching patient confidentiality, the results of our collective efforts, not in an abstract and theoretical manner, unconvincing to those left out of the process, but rather as part of a truthful exchange about our experiences with the child, focusing on daily life in the areas of training, education and therapy.

We shall see when we review the concepts of institutional psychotherapy that all this work can only be accomplished through major reorganisation of the treatment team.

On Babies

Although these considerations concern above all patients with archaic disorders, another group of patients can also benefit from them greatly: babies.

Let us take the example of a nursery. When a professional encounters a problem in his work with a baby, most often it has to do with something that is bothering the baby. Of course, the latter is not aware of the difficulties of those around him; his limited means (crying, screams, sleep and feeding disturbances . . .) of signalling them must be well-known to early childhood professionals, so that they may find an appropriate solution. In most cases, an experienced professional eventually understands what the baby needs, and finds a way to satisfy him. But sometimes he is unable to do this and finds himself in a difficult – even embarrassing – situation. If he has the opportunity to speak with the other professionals, he can discuss his dilemma. Another professional caring for the same baby might for example state that he has no such difficulties with the baby. In many teams, the fact that someone says: "With me, everything goes well" immediately makes the professional who spoke of his problem feel devalued, even if no one comments. But the discomfort becomes unbearable when the professional who encountered none of the problems his colleague had, or a superior, or the team leader insists on the professional inadequacy of the person who spoke of his difficulties openly. It is as if the latter is told: "No wonder you have problems; you don't have proper qualifications". This official reproach becomes a judgement, a sort of inquisition, and the professional who wanted to benefit from his colleagues' advice in order to do better with the baby finds himself embroiled in a process that leads to loss of self-worth, and eventually to depression and possible burnout.

But if we view this example from a different perspective, other aspects of the work come to light and contribute to a clearer understanding of this baby, and therefore of the care he receives in the nursery.

The professional who has a problem gives his opinion about his relationship with the baby. Other professionals describe their relationship with him, and the meeting reveals that this baby seems to get along with certain caregivers but has a difficult relationship with others. Instead of concluding at once that the former are good professionals while the latter are incompetent, it is interesting to consider, "in principle", that each professional is competent but embodies the place he holds in the familial constellation transposed to the nursery.

In the case presented here, the nursery director has noticed for some time that the baby's parents do not seem to be getting along. Several times she witnessed smoldering conflict between them during meetings she or the nursery paediatrician had scheduled with them. One day, with tears in her eyes, the mother told the paediatrician and those present that her husband had become distant with her and paid little attention to the baby. She was terrified that her husband would leave her and was sure it was just a matter of time. The professionals' reports, viewed in light of this information, took on an entirely different meaning: for the baby, some of the professionals hold a reassuring and calming position, similar to that of the mother; with them, the everyday routine is relatively peaceful. The other professionals obviously hold a more distressing position, closer to that of the father; with them, the baby's experiences of the father's changing attitudes are revealed through difficulties in the daily routine.

As we can see, the conclusions drawn in the first type of meeting are very different than those produced by the second type of meeting. In the first case, sweeping judgement can have dramatic consequences on professionals, without helping the baby or his parents in the least. In the second scenario, not only is the team the setting for what is played out between the baby and his parents, but in addition, the clarifications resulting from the analysis of the events discussed in the meeting will incite the professionals at the nursery to go over these events with the parents, to help them realise what is at stake.

As a matter of fact, in this example, the outcome was not what had been expected, for the mother's fear of separation was only an expression of a depression into which she had sunk weeks earlier, and which had caused her to drive the father away from the baby almost without him noticing it, producing the clinical picture we described earlier. The work which followed this meeting made it possible, in ways useful to the baby, to his parents and to the professionals involved, to take steps towards resolving a problem crucial for the baby, and to improve his relations with his parents and caregivers. This example shows that the transferential constellation can apply to babies and benefit them and their parents, as well as the team to which they have been referred.

My extensive experience in consultation-liaison child psychiatry in Neonatology, Paediatrics and Maternity departments has shown me that many situations involving newborns, babies, small children or problematic parent-baby relations can benefit from this "institutional" approach.

On Dependent Persons

In more general terms, all individuals who experience difficulties in their relations with others, and especially people who find themselves in a situation of extreme dependence,[16] bring into play psychopathological mechanisms very amenable to the benefits offered by the transferential constellation. We shall see that often the concept of "complementary relations" (Eugène Dupréel) can enrich that of transferential constellation. Indeed, in addition to the caregivers involved on a daily basis, all the professionals treating these disorders benefit from coming together to share their different perspectives on the patient[17] and specify the nature of their interactions with him. This can reveal that the functions presumably carried out by these caregivers do not coincide with the roles they actually play. Complementarity is what allows these different functions to exert their collective effect.

Notes

1 Schotte, J., *Vers l'anthropopsychiatrie. Un parcours*, Paris: Hermann, 2008.
2 Schotte, J., *Szondi avec Freud. Sur la voie d'une psychiatrie pulsionnelle*, Brussels: De Boeck, 1992.

3 Schotte, J. (Ed.), *Le contact*, Brussels: De Boeck, 1992.
4 Ibid., p. 11.
5 Mélon, J., "De l'école hongroise de psychanalyse à Szondi et à la psychiatrie d'aujourd'hui", in Schotte, J. (Ed.), op. cit., p. 21.
6 Delion, P., *L'enfant autiste, le bébé et la sémiotique* (The Autistic Child, the Baby and Semiotics), Paris: PUF, 2000.
7 Maldiney, H., *Regard, parole, espace* (Gaze, Speech, Space), Lausanne: L'Âged'homme, 1973.
8 Ibid., p. 70.
9 Deledalle, G., *Charles S. Pierce's Philosophy of Signs*, Bloomington, Indiana: Indiana University Press, 2000, pp. 67–68.
10 Ibid., p. 70.
11 Maldiney, H., *Regard, parole, espace*, Paris: Le Cerf, 2012.
12 Ibid., pp. 136–138.
13 Ayme, J., "Attitude interprétative dans le transfert en psychothérapie institutionelle", *Psychology Institute* 1, 1965.
14 Racamier, P.-C., *Le psychanalyste sans divan*, Paris: Payot, 1970.
15 Oury, J., *Le Collectif. Séminaire de Sainte-Anne*, Paris: Scarabée, 1986.
16 Négrel, M.-F., "La clinique de la rue", *Empan* 96, 2014, pp. 57–59.
17 In compliance with medical confidentiality and applicable professional secrecy.

Chapter 6

Institutional Psychotherapy
A Review

Why Go Back to the Beginning?

The transferential constellation is a concept dating back to the founders of this radical movement in psychiatry born in the second half of the 20th century. This concept might be said to be the smallest common denominator linking the reforms introduced by this movement.

We shall therefore go over the axioms constituting the concept, to present the elements which define it to the contemporary reader. The fact is that institutional psychotherapy is one of the theoretical and practical forms of psychiatry which will undoubtedly reveal its usefulness again in these times when oversimplifying managerial ideologies predominate and there is a strong tendency towards rigid classification and fragmented definition, which will lead to the predictable return of practice once widespread in asylums, affecting hospitalised patients and their freedom of circulation.

One of our colleagues, Alain Buzaré – departed too soon – chose as the title of his book Jean Oury's emblematic definition: "Institutional psychotherapy is what psychiatry is".[1] Today, it appears that psychiatry needs to return to the humanistic and civilising foundations it lost over the past few decades due to the emergence of a science-based perspective reducing Man to the sum of his organic components, despite the humanistic psychotherapy introduced after the war through the creation of institutional psychotherapy and sectorised psychiatry.

We often forget that historically the creation of asylums, often criticised and even regarded with contempt today, constituted a considerable advance by providing specific places where mentally ill patients could "receive care from skilled physicians" who applied the psychological treatment invented by Pinel in the spirit of 18th-century Enlightenment. Article 1 of the 1838 law regarding the insane (now called "mentally

DOI: 10.4324/9781003380269-6

ill") stipulated that "every county is required to have a public institution specifically designed to welcome and treat the insane". This was the start of a new, humanistic psychiatry. But the history of psychiatry in the 19th century was marked by much turmoil, and asylums increasingly became places of confinement and mistreatment of the mentally ill – a painful episode in our history. Looking back, the fact that the asylum was part of the era Foucault described as "the great confinement" can be attributed to the absence of the concept that Freud would develop and designate by the general term "transferential relation". This is not to say that the Freudian invention of "transference", intended to establish an appropriate distance vis-à-vis neurotic patients and to help them overcome their difficulties, was sufficient to avoid entropic institutional risks, but rather that the concepts proposed by the post-Freudians regarding the effects of transference of the mentally ill on the psychic life and the behaviour of their caregivers were elucidated by the notion of "transferential relations".

Today, the greatest misunderstanding concerns the diagnostic gap between ordinary Western neuroses and the more severe archaic disorders, and thus between different forms of treatment. This could cause the critics of psychoanalysis to consign it to the dustbin of history. Indeed, the mission of psychiatry is to treat the mentally ill. But since Freud, neurotics have joined the ranks of the "normosed" (Ayme), except when severe symptoms threaten the autonomy of the subject. Psychoanalysts have focused on these psychopathologies and treated them successfully in many cases, conferring them legitimacy.

By contrast, major disorders like schizophrenia, autism, the manic-depressive psychoses, emotional deprivation and other borderline pathologies, which were the focus of numerous psychoanalytic studies and therapies, were never cured by means of psychoanalysis – at least as far as I know. With a few exceptions, it was always necessary to provide a specific space for these patients, be it for the duration of their treatment or temporarily. And it is precisely in this symbolic space that psychiatry and its "institutions" exert their crucial function.

But we have seen that although the foundations of institutional psychotherapy were laid with great expectations by Pinel and Pussin, Esquirol's initiative, when he founded the asylum, did not produce the expected results, even though this specific space should have served to obtain them. In fact, some of the reasons for this failure were only elucidated by Freudian concepts invented later. But despite the birth of psychoanalysis, and specifically of the notion of transference, institutional entropy continued into the 20th century, up until the Second World War, without improving the fate of the most seriously ill patients, but on the contrary, causing the death by starvation of 45,000 patients hospitalised in psychiatric institutions in France between 1939 and 1945.

It would take a combination of major events (the Spanish Civil War, the Second World War, the fight against Nazi ideology, the encounter of a few historical figures in the world of psychiatry and a favorable political juncture) for the pioneers of what would become institutional psychotherapy to set in place this practice of humanistic psychiatry successfully. What was needed was to transform psychiatric establishments into places adapted to psychopathological disorders, where the disenfranchised could be admitted and treated with respect, regardless of their medical condition.

A Little History

Like many republicans, Tosquelles[2] fled Catalonia, where he had worked as a psychiatrist at the Pere Mata de Reus Hospital since 1935 and had also been appointed psychiatric head of the republican army, to escape the death sentence issued by the Franco regime. In France, he was initially "held" at the Septfonds concentration camp for several months before being found by French colleagues who suggested that he come to Saint-Alban with his family. When he arrived at the Lozère psychiatric hospital in January 1940, he brought with him two books which were to guide his practice and his reflection: Lacan's thesis on the Aimée case (1932), which had been translated into Spanish in 1933, and a work by Hermann Simon, director of the Gütersloh psychiatric hospital, in which the author recommends "active work therapy in the psychiatric hospital". Seeing a new form of psychiatry emerging from the practices that had been used in asylums, and with the help of Paul Balvet, his wife Germaine and a few motivated caregivers, Tosquelles undertook the systematic transformation of the Saint-Alban hospital, relying on the lessons learned during his training at the Reus hospital in Catalonia under Mira y Lopez,[3] the lessons learned in Barcelona in his analysis with Sandor Eminder, a student of Ferenczi – another Jew who emigrated from Budapest – as well as the lessons learned while he fought in the Spanish Civil War as a member of the Workers' Party of Marxist Unification[4] and psychiatrist of the republican army.

Rather than introducing the standard psychoanalytic treatment model into the hospital setting, and after serious reflection in light of his war experiences[5] and his Marxist culture, Tosquelles decided to enrich the psychopathological perspective with the contributions psychoanalysis had to offer, by constructing a new metapsychology that could be extended to psychotic disorders.[6] To do this, he relied not only on psychoanalytic writing already known by Spanish psychiatrists, who translated German and English psychiatric and psychoanalytic texts as soon as they were published – which was not the case in France – but also on other sources such as Mira y Lopez, his psychiatry professor in Reus, and Hermann Simon, who insisted that the practice must see to it that patients are not left to wallow in their morbid lack of activity, and must make it a priority to see to the health of the hospital before attempting to treat patients.

Before long, anthropological and sociopolitical research with a wider scope emerged from the intense discussions about Saint-Alban, which Tosquelles held with the Gévaudan professional group created with Lucien Bonnafé when the latter was appointed director of the hospital at the end of 1942.

Institutional psychotherapy is said to be supported by two pillars: psychoanalysis and the political.

The Therapeutic Club

The psychiatric practice founded at Saint-Alban during World War II, and reinforced in the years that followed, made it possible to introduce a treatment device of a radically different nature, deriving from the 1901 Law of Associations: the therapeutic club. The club is managed by the patients themselves, with some supervision provided by caregivers. This means that patients take responsibility for organising their daily lives, and also promote access to cultural activities and social events. This vector of change invented by Tosquelles[7] and later adopted by many groups thanks to the decree issued on February 5th, 1958, constituted a formidable tool for the transformation of psychiatric hospitals, since it gave patients the means of participating in the cooperative organisation of their own daily lives under certain conditions.

In Tosquelles's view, this constituted applying to mental illness the humanist principle illustrated by Freud's crystal, on the assumption that there is no structural difference between patients and caregivers, all of them being located on a continuum between normal and pathological. But it is also a concept made famous by Kleinian analysis, the concept of the "good portion": every human being has a healthy portion on which he can rely with the help of the therapist while healing his unhealthy portion. Moreover, this position obviously presents a powerful political dimension, opposed to segregation, and in radical contrast with the ideology of the Nazis, who had introduced a program for the elimination of the mentally ill (the T4 Program) in 1934. In addition, the therapeutic club is a device that can only function if it relies on all the practices of the group, thereby enhancing the effects of individual treatment as it had been delivered previously.

The Meetings

For the ground-breaking innovation creating the therapeutic clubs to be successful, several new practices were introduced, particularly the meeting bringing patients and caregivers together. This revolutionised relations between the two groups, which were often opposed in the past. These meetings proved to exert a very useful collective effect. Participants were able to speak freely without fear of reprimand by the hierarchical system. Although today it is clear that meetings are an integral part of organising human groups, at the time Tosquelles[8] and his friends in Saint-Alban had to work hard to set them in place. In a famous article, Jean Oury developed the theoretical concept of the meeting.[9] The means which rendered these advances possible include one element Oury always emphasised: the training of the personnel.

Institutional Psychotherapy and Sectorised Psychiatry

The experiment carried out in this rural hospital during the war led to profound changes in psychiatric practices by turning patients into actors of their lives in the institution, with the help of caregivers trained in institutional psychotherapy, and by developing a practice that would play an important role in psychiatric research after 1945: the practice of releasing patients from the hospital and conducting a follow-up of their activities. This link between hospital activities and activities outside the hospital would become the matrix of sectorised psychiatry, defining the conditions of a patient's treatment possibilities for the entire duration of his treatment. Another advantage of these innovative practices was the fact that not a single patient died of starvation at Saint-Alban, while in France during the same sinister period, 45,000 mentally ill patients perished. At Saint-Alban, certain patients could leave the hospital to take part in socially valued activities (craftmanship, rural labor), contributing to food supplies for the hospital and preventing the death from starvation of the most dependent patients. Moreover, it became evident that the patients who worked outside the hospital were not only carrying out a rescue mission for the others but had found in this activity[10] a way to escape their mental illness to some degree, applying in a more cooperative fashion the work therapy concept originally introduced by Tosquelles. After the war, when national solidarity was crucially important, the experiment conducted in this hospital would become one of the models for a new psychiatry based on unprecedented principles. Soon, all these experiments paved the way for a new, humanistic psychiatry, deliberately distinct from a hospital-centred model, favoring instead a community-oriented model designed to meet the needs of patients and their families in the community at large. A psychiatric care team is made available to a segment of the population – that of a geodemographic sector – and provides treatment to patients as long as they need it. This team works with specifically designed treatment tools, the hospital department being just one link in the chain, along with mental health clinics (based on the model of the social services agencies invented under the Popular Front[11] regime), prevention and consultation centres, follow-up centres and part-time hospitals.

The principles that founded the ground-breaking work at Saint-Alban and are the very essence of institutional psychotherapy also constitute its framework, while the geodemographic sector makes their application possible. The fundamental axis of this revolution is the implementation of procedures allowing the follow-up of the most severely ill patients as long as necessary, through what the 1960 circular (March 15) establishing sectorised psychiatry called "continuity in care". Of course, it is clear that this possibility offered to treatment teams originates directly from the Freudian concept of "transference", modified to apply, as Tosquelles applied it, to pathologies other than neuroses. Sectorised psychiatry was established in the 1970s and, in some places at least, continued to use concepts borrowed from institutional psychotherapy. However, in many teams, the influence exerted by antipsychiatry created an ambiguous relation with the notion of institutional psychotherapy, attributing to its proponents hospital-centred intentions contrary to its founding theories and practices: it was as if the need to add hospital beds to the wide range of treatment solutions were proof of hidden hospital-centrism. But the fact is that psychiatry cannot do without these means unless it leaves to others the "treatment" of the most serious cases.

Two Social and Psychopathological Forms of Alienation

The notion of double alienation is extremely important in Jean Oury's work, since from a certain point of view it establishes the need for institutions. The mentally ill individual suffers from two types of insanity: social and psychopathological.

Indeed, a patient with delusions or subject to depression is made to suffer by these symptoms which lead to a psychiatric diagnosis. But the existence of this particular type of suffering also subjects the patient to the scrutiny of his social circle, which in most cases excludes him. He is either minimally excluded by reason of his depression, stops working and feels guilty for being dependent on those who support him; or he is excluded altogether because of his delusions, rejected by a social milieu that does not tolerate madmen in its midst. These two effects should not be confused, for misconstruing them could lead to inappropriate responses in terms of the treatment offered to the patient.

The proponents of antipsychiatry thought that society caused fragile people to become mentally ill, and they contributed to eliminating facilities for psychiatric hospitalisation. Alienists thought that society had nothing to do with it and duplicated in their asylums the same rejection mechanisms as those previously in existence in human communities. It is essential to consider the two forms of insanity in order to design devices that allow a relevant response. Sectorised psychiatry and institutional psychotherapy constitute a model enabling a coherent response to double alienation.

Thanks to his in-depth analysis of the concept of double alienation, Oury helps us understand the radical difference between various arguments against letting a patient spend all his time hospitalised, once his psychopathological illness is sufficiently taken into account, but without providing follow-up for as long as he needs, since the reasons for his social alienation often continue to apply to his life as a citizen marginalised by his psychopathological alienation.

Given that they served as an excuse, the anti-psychiatric measures taken against institutional psychotherapy are responsible in large part for the reduction of means granted for the development of sectorised psychiatry. Indeed, technocrats viewed these ideological positions with cynicism: the idea of eliminating psychiatric beds provided a perfect opportunity to economise on hospitalisation space, and consequently on spending dedicated to psychiatry.

In addition, psychiatrists only interested in the neurosciences do not take social alienation into account and ignore many problems the patient cannot solve alone. At times, some psychiatrists decide to undertake information campaigns addressed to the general public, to spread the idea that mental illness is a disease like any other. But we know very well that this can have no profound effect on an "ordinary" citizen.

Revival or Predictable Demise of Institutional Psychotherapy?

Despite having divided into opposing strands, institutional psychotherapy continued to exist in many psychiatric departments, gradually transforming the practice of psychiatry itself. I cannot cite here all the departments involved, but I refer the reader to several works which attempt to provide an exhaustive list; one of them[12] in particular describes the work of numerous teams involved in this process of change, including at the international level.

Recently, a change seems to be taking place again. Caregivers are taking an interest in institutional psychotherapy, which has long been believed to be out of favour. As far back as 1982, after the publication of an article by Philippe Koechlin[13] announcing the demise of institutional psychotherapy, when I suggested that *L'information psychiatrique* publish a double issue[14] on the subject to include the very many contributions showing that it was alive and well, I felt as if I lived on another planet and was talking about a strange type of psychiatry for which I sought the support of my colleagues. This feeling stemmed from the widening distance between the practices based on this psychiatric movement – institutional psychotherapy – and the practices already influenced by a form of idealised antipsychiatry which tended to perpetuate life in the asylum, making technocrats happy, so much so that it could be supposed that they had determined its content.

But since 1983, the gap has become a wider chasm than I ever thought I would have to cross as a result of the speedy deconstruction of this humanistic psychiatry.

Still, we must pay tribute to Philippe Koechlin, who left us in 2010 and was the inventor of the term "institutional psychotherapy", used for the first time in an article coauthored with Georges Daumezon for the *Annaïs Portuguese* in 1952. Koechlin strove to apply the principles of this psychiatry wherever he worked. Most importantly, he and Edmée Koechlin coauthored a small book, *Corridor de sécurité*,[15] published by Maspero, which I still consider the description of a crucial experimental application of this psychiatry. At this juncture of urgency and crisis, the actors concerned should draw inspiration from this book to avert a probable return to locked-door psychiatric wards, for the sake of security.

Today, a great deal is at stake and renewed interest in this movement could bring unexpected answers to unsolved questions in psychiatry, such as why are there still hospitals for the mentally ill? Rather than being discouraged, should we not consider the possibility of creating humane places where these patients can come when they need to? Is the only thing they need hospitalisation in psychiatry, or rather teams of dynamic people always ready to be there for them when they go through inevitable psychic storms?

Establishment and Institution

This is where the concept of "institution" acquires its undisputed importance. What is an institution? Tosquelles always differentiated the establishment from the institution. The former is created by the State to provide answers to the major problems to which a human society is confronted. The institution, on the other hand, is the way in which a team of professionals "occupies" an establishment, adapting to the specific contextual requirements imposed on it. In psychiatry, the French mental health law of 1938 created asylums in every county, and later the 1960 Circular divided them into geodemographic sectors. The population of each sector was to receive psychiatric care from a team combining social services with mental health care. One or several medico-psychological centres would be created to diagnose and treat pathologies with the help of a range of treatment tools such as outpatient clinics, part-time or full-time hospitals, home visits, etc. But each sector team was free to invent the devices most suited to the needs and resources in its assigned sector in order to respond optimally to every situation. Contrary to what we might assume at first glance, this sectorial device operates according to principles compatible with institutional psychotherapy, since individual situations must be examined collectively to find relevant solutions. This involves meetings, looking at clinical cases in a psychopathological light, dealing with inevitable institutional divisions, collaborating with the other professionals in the network centred on the person who needs help and making it possible for each patient to meet with individual care-givers and with the team.

Institutional Psychotherapy and the Transferential Constellation

But what has become of institutional psychotherapies as such? I speak of them in the plural because a whole set of practices are designated as institutional psychotherapy, although they take as many different forms as there are teams to apply them. I see this as a fundamental sign of the usefulness of this practice, since each team can refer to the same general principles while developing a particular style that depends on the char-acteristics of its members, on the historical context and on many other factors.

We have seen many teams create remarkable practices based on a variety of principles, such as the La Borde clinic (Oury), the ASM13 Centre (Paumelle), the Mental Health and Communities Association (Guyotat and Hochmann) in Villeurbane, in Orléans,[16] in Reims (Patrick Chemla), in Angers (Denis and Bonnal), in Landerneau (Le Roux, de Chaizemartin), in Besançon (Racamier), in Mareille (Tosquellas, Vian-der and Abrieu), in Abbeville (Chaperot), in Caen (Grété), in Asnières,[17] the Children's Day Hospital in Paris (Moya Plama and Giroux), the

Rehabilitation Follow-up Centre in Château Rauzé (Richer and Balat) and many others.

It is also worthwhile to mention experiments in institutional education,[18] very similar to those in institutional psychotherapy. In this welcome diversity, the transferential constellation has remained the common element shared by different practices.

Presuming that the institution is created by a team, to be implemented in a humane fashion in a space of care, and that the psychotherapy of patients other than those presenting neuroses cannot limit itself to standard therapy, institutional psychotherapy, in a sector or a group, is the sum of the transferential constellations of each patient and of institutions making room for everyone, to fulfil different needs (a therapeutic club, a newspaper, a cultural association . . .).

We have seen that the transferential constellation is the group of people in contact with a patient whose transference process is "dissociative" (Oury) or "adhesive", or "projective" when the group constitutes a collective protective shield and performs a containing function. The constellation can only exist thanks to meetings of the group but needs more than these meetings. It fills a function of "continuity of being" (Winnicott) in each caregiver's countertransference, creating what Tosquelles called "institutional countertransference". In order to safeguard this delicate weave, we cannot underestimate the importance department heads must grant to all questions of power rivalry constantly at work in human communities.

Statutory Hierarchy and Subjectal Hierarchy

Today, the role of a department head mainly involves attempting to be a technobureaucratic "dam against the Pacific",[19] to allow for emergence downstream of the culture needed for the psychic survival of the actors of the therapeutic enterprise, and consequently for the psychic sustainment of the patients. The reference to Marguerite Duras's book underscores the exhausting and futile character of the fantasy of effective resistance against the deconstruction of the spaces of mental health care in the current power struggle, especially since "new management"[20] has replaced previous models of "personnel management". In this context, I suggest that we distinguish statutory hierarchy, which serves to organise the "official" functioning of teams in an establishment, from subjectal hierarchy, which can take into account archaic transference in the treatment of persons presenting psychopathological neglect.

Statutory hierarchy can exist where there is no subjectal hierarchy, and things will proceed with no apparent difficulty. In this situation the transferential relation is ignored, caregivers are interchangeable and the resulting efficiency can keep things afloat in the best of cases, but has entropic effects most of the time. Indeed, in most cases the vicissitudes of transference become evident. In general, they emerge in the form of acting out on the part of one or the other of those involved. But if the health care professionals decide – since a decision is needed – to take transference into account, then subjectal hierarchy must exist as well.

Free Circulation, Free Expression

But all this is not enough to allow free circulation of unconstrained speech[21] between the members of the caregiving team; it only creates the possibility of its existence in certain favorable conditions. "Democracy is the worst form of government – except for all the others", Churchill said, because it allows free circulation of ideas and individuals, something authoritarian or totalitarian regimes do not allow. And indeed, the mode of governance of the new *management* places it among such regimes. Yet the history of psychiatry has shown us, in regard to mentally ill patients described as alienated, that freedom of circulation is needed to carry out the work of their disalienation.

In doing this work, Oury's concept of "atmosphere" proves extremely useful, since it allows us to describe the "atmospheric" environment needed by a team of professionals to encourage them to come together in transferential constellations as often as necessary. If their desire is "made operational"[22] and supported by a statutory hierarchy respectful of the initiatives of each team member, creating a transversality[23] conducive to the emergence of a subjectal hierarchy, a new adventure can begin, so that facilitating the expression of countertransferential experiences can lead to a narrative and representational function of the patient's story in connection with one's own world. Oury insisted on the importance of a transferential reading of the events in a patient's daily life in light of his subjective history. All these necessary elements connected together based on transferential reasoning constitute what Hélène Chaigneau[24] so nicely called "just enough" in the long-term care of patients with serious psychopathologies.

Complementary Relations

It is also interesting to realise that the caregivers are engaged in complementary relations[25] with contacts in the community. In order for a patient to feel real improvement in his psychic state, it is helpful for him to be accompanied by the caregiving team, but often this is insufficient if he also needs help with his physical health, or help from a social worker (housing, family, work . . .). All these professionals have a role to play, and here too we observe that if there is, in fact, complementarity, the beneficial effects are much greater. On the other hand, if each person sees himself as playing the crucial role and sees the other partners as accessory, division is introduced, as it inevitably is in ego rivalry, and the intended objective suffers. In such situations, problems generally associated with narcissistic perversion often arise.[26] Contrary to this foreseeable entropic disorganisation, the patient needs several kinds of competencies to be exercised around him to help him overcome his difficulties. This reasoning is essential in the treatment of archaic pathologies and goes hand in hand with the concept of transferential constellation.

When dealing with children presenting ASDs, the modes of intervention I recommend to parents, "educational always, pedagogical if possible and therapeutic if necessary", emerged from reflection on the logic of complementarities that can help the child in his development. This recommendation is based directly on complementary relations. Indeed, the first element – "educational always" – is undeniable. Obviously, parents are the educators of their children. Sometimes, in certain circumstances, a child's specific need forces the parents to modify their educational skills. For instance, a child might be deaf. As soon as the diagnosis is made, it will be suggested that the parents learn sign language, so that their child can have a means of communicating with them. They are not replaced in their role as educators; instead, they acquire new skills with the help of specialised educators who teach them sign language. The parents of an autistic child are often in a very difficult situation because this pathology prevents the very possibility of intersubjectivity and eliminates the means of communicating with the child. Often, the parents go through a period of doubt – which they don't always overcome – when they question whether they are good parents. Some become depressed, others feel guilty. When they come to see us, we are often the first to be made aware of these deeply repressed feelings of loss of self-worth, manifesting as depression and discouragement. This clinical state of the parents, whom causalist minds misguidedly deem responsible for autism, shows that these parents need personal help to have the strength to be and to remain the educators they wish to be. In these situations, it can be useful for parents to seek help from educators specialising in autism, in order to learn techniques that allow them to establish contact with their child. In my practice, I ask the parents what they think is useful for the child. They then tell me about methods they heard about from other people, in the media or described on specialised sites. No matter what these methods are, if the parents judge them to be useful, they are the ones suited to their child, until more is known.

The second element –"pedagogical if possible" – is schooling. Contrary to what has long been said and done, I feel it is important that an autistic child receive learning, as long as the teacher adapts the teaching to the child's particular abilities and the resources of the environment are taken into account. For example, a 3-year-old child can attempt going to school; if no new difficulties are encountered, it would have been regrettable to deprive him of the experience. Often, teachers ask parents to make special arrangements allowing easier integration in the classroom: a special-needs assistant for the child, a teaching assistant, enrolment in specialised programs, etc. In some cases, the child's intellectual level and the seriousness of his pathology do not allow him to benefit from being in an ordinary classroom. In that case, he has to attend a medico-social establishment. Finally, a child's clinical state of anxiety can be such that the only thing to do is for him to go to the day hospital of his paedopsychiatric sector, where he will find not only specialised care, but also teaching provided by the Ministry of Education, which carries out the pedagogical function within the caregiving team and in cooperation with its members.

The third element – "therapeutic if necessary" – will only be implemented if the first two do not provide adequate support for the autistic child in his family and at school: for instance, when the parents, during their regular visits with us, speak of the persistence or return of autism-specific problems, archaic fears . . . A child does rather well at school but eating remains a problem at home and each meal causes destructuring anxiety which not only torments him but disturbs the whole family. Another child seems to benefit from educational assistance at home but shows signs of troubling anxiety at school, in the form of uncontrollable stereotypes or even self-mutilation. Yet another child shows, through more frequent reactions of retreating, active underlying anxieties depriving him of the possibility of being with others, in his family as well as at school. In these cases, I recommend stays in the day hospital, either for as short a period as possible if integration in school can continue without much difficulty, or full-time if the child suffers from severe anxiety requiring long-term therapy.

When therapy is initiated, the first stage consists of observing the child in different situations, to identify the factors which provoke the emergence of anxiety, as well as those which help to appease it. This allows us to create a sort of "Map of Tendre" of the child, which helps us to distinguish the circumstances in which these fears indicate the failure of the child's usual defences and are inevitably expressed in ways that can be extreme.

After this, we draw up a plan of care, a sort of made-to-measure therapeutic suit based on all our observations at the hospital, as well as the observations conveyed by the parents. We have seen that the children can then rely on the support of caregivers to go through the stages that help them overcome these painful moments and regain competencies already acquired, to go on with their development. But for this method to be useful and effective, the participants from these three different spheres of experience must be able to work together, and to include the parents as well. The concept of complementary relations refers precisely to this complex institutional interaction.

Layout of Daily Life and the Three Phoric Functions

Institutional psychotherapy is a mode of thinking and practice which sees everyday life as a layout on which the evolution of a patient in an unstable psychopathological state inscribes the actions designating his need, transforming it gradually into a personal story told in the first person singular. The time-spaces dedicated to following this evolution constitute opportunities to be accompanied, carried, held, supported – what I propose calling a "phoric function",[27] if we agree to give this name to Winnicottien "holding": carrying the patient on one's psychic shoulders for the entire time he needs until he can, hopefully, become independent. This means that if dependence is a permanent state, this function can last a lifetime; this would greatly alter the project of the team, as compared to its present focus on "emergencies". But this first stage is not enough. Contact with the patient allows caregivers to be open to that patient's particular transference and to become, often unknowingly, the carriers of his psychic suffering – a semaphoric function. When we carry out this function, we place our psychic apparatus at the disposal of the patient, allowing elements of his psychopathology to develop there, although they are not without effect on the psyches of caregivers. The concept of countertransference is elucidated by Salomon Resnik, who introduced the notion of "double transference"[28] to draw attention to the subtle intersubjective dialectic at play here. The transferential constellation meetings concerning that patient are opportunities to discuss each person's countertransference/double transference, so that sometimes an understanding, a meaning or an indication emerges: this is the metaphoric function, whose primary effect is to shed a different light on clinical reality. The experience described by Freud in *Jokes and Their Relation to the Unconscious*,[29] "bewilderment and enlightenment", is where the psychic apparatus of the caregivers involved in this exceptional human relationship will find the means to reorganise itself when interacting with the patient thereafter. At the same time, this experience reduces the caregiver's degree of suffering, whereas if this suffering is ignored, it can lead to burnout.[30]

We do not fully realise the extent to which, for a caregiver in psychiatry, his participation in the transferential adventure, which requires extreme generosity, can also give him intellectual and emotional satisfactions which validate his choice of this singular profession. This is what I call the "Balint Function",[31] a concept I often use to explain the effects of transferential constellation meetings attended by professionals, regardless of their status. In these meetings, participants discuss, in a manner similar to the method Balint applied with general medicine practitioners, the vicissitudes of caregiving relations, particularly in the long term. The specific effects on each caregiver's subjective position are facilitated by this approach, provided that his participation in encouraged by his hierarchy.

Secure Psychiatry or Safe Institutional Psychotherapy?

My insistence on the necessary distinction between statutory and subjective hierarchies is a question of great concern, closely related to the present misguided reactions observed even at the highest level of government concerning the appropriate response when a team meets with failure: the head of the team has to be sanctioned. The word "sanction" becomes the response of Old Man Whipper to all difficulties encountered, with no questioning of what might have led to the failure. These types of mediametric considerations transform decision makers into righteous sermonisers ("If it had happened to me, I would have known what to do!"), infantilizing the individuals involved ("I am surrounded by incompetent people") and falsely claiming that any complex problem can have a simple solution – which is diametrically opposed to the position of a legally accountable person, a position necessary for humble and modest participation in the community of humankind. In the present context of maximum reinforcement of security, particularly in the field of psychiatry, the appeal launched by the actors of the institutional psychotherapy movement to members of caregiving groups prompting them to assume a "desiring" position in their work, in favour of free circulation of speech ensuing from the free circulation of individuals, creativity and the invention of made-to-measure therapeutic methods for each patient, relative self-management in regard to the tools needed to implement psychiatric care – this appeal summarises the ethical positions enabling these practices and the theorisations needed for *safe* psychiatry.[32]

If the measures taken to deal with a small number of people in trouble with the law (pushed to regrettable extremes by their psychopathology, sometimes even as far as murder) become the dominant position demanded of those who work in psychiatry, the minimal conditions that institutional psychotherapy see as better tools will not be in place, and the entire sphere of psychiatry will become security-centred. But what we need is safe psychiatry, not secure psychiatry. Given the very high incidence of mental illness, the actors of the psychiatric profession cannot tolerate seeing the framework of their practice become asylum-like once again based on demagogic arguments, knowing that sectorised psychiatry using institutional psychotherapy methods has clearly shown its effectiveness. We cannot accept such a regression and we must strive to make decision makers understand that locking people up is contrary to the essential principles of democracy. But perhaps a pseudo-democracy on a media-like model[33] has already caused the citizens and their representatives to forget the relevance of the fabled phrase: "A society should be judged . . . by how it treats its criminals [and the mentally ill]". Institutional psychotherapy showed us methods of improving the treatment of these patients. Now, it must mount resistance once again, to combat the threat of the deconstruction of humanist psychiatry and must reconstitute teams which wish to practice it. Patients, their families and the professionals engaged in this work cannot tolerate indefinitely a "veterinary" approach (without exchange of words) to mental illness.

Notes

1 Buzaré, A., *La psychothérapie institutionnelle, c'est la psychiatrie*, Nîmes: Éditions du champ social, 2002.
2 Tosquellas, J., *Francesc Tosquelles: Psychiatre, Catalan, Marxiste*, Édition d'une, 2021.
3 The first professor of psychiatry, named by the republicans, at the Faculty of Medecine in Barcelona in 1934.
4 Marxist workers' party, formerly the Iberian Communist Federation.
5 Bion, like Tosquelles, was to enrich his psychoanalytic experience considerably during World War II, with experiments in group psychotherapy.
6 Tosquelles's first concern at Saint-Alban were the children – many of them psychotic – hospitalised at Villaret, for whom he developed the same treatment strategy as that for adults.

7 Tosquelles presented an initial report on therapeutic clubs at the 1952 Croix-Marine Conference in Pau, before a decree and a newsletter made the Therapeutic Club official in February 1958, thanks to the decision of Félix Houphouët-Boigny, minister of Public Health and Population.

8 Tosquelles, F., *De la personne au groupe*, Toulouse: érès, 1995.

9 Oury, J., "Existe-t-il un concept de réunion?", in *Psychiatrie et psychothérapie institutionnelle*, Nîmes: Éditions du champ social, 2003.

10 Tosquelles, F., *Le travail thérapeutique à l'hôpital psychiatrique*, Paris: Éditions du Scarabée, 1967; *Le travail thérapeutique en psychiatrie*, Toulouse: érès, 2009.

11 See 1937 *Circular of the Minister of Health*, Marc Rucart.

12 Delion, P. (Ed.), *Actualité de la psychothérapie institutionnelle*, Vigneux: Matrice, 1991.

13 Koechlin, P., "La mort de la psychothérapie institutionnelle", *L'information psychiatrique*, no. 8, 1982.

14 Delion, P. (Ed.), "Psychothérapie institutionnelle", *L'information psychiatrique*, no. 3 and 4, 1983.

15 Koechlin, E. & P., *Corridor de sécurité*, Paris: Maspero, 1974; Éditions d'une, 2019.

16 Fauregas, P., Gentis, R., Oury, J., *L'arrière-pays. Aux sources de la psychothérapie institutionnelle*, Toulouse: érès, 2020; Torrubia, H., *La psychothérapie institutionnelle par gros temps*, Nimes: Éditions Champ Social, 2002.

17 Bellahsen, M., Kanebel, R., Bellahsen, L., *La révolte de la psychiatrie*, Paris: La Découverte, 2020.

18 Oury, F., Vasquez, A., *Vers une pédagogie institutionnelle*, Paris: Maspero, 1977.

19 Duras, M., *Un barrage contre le Pacifique* (A Dam Against the Pacific), Paris: Gallimard, 1950.

20 Chapoutot, J., *Free to Obey*, Rendall, S. (Trans.), New York: Europa Compass, 2022.

21 Lacan, J., "The Function of Speech and Language in Psychoanalysis", in *Écrits: A Selection*, New York: W. W. Norton, 1977.

22 Legrand, M., *Léopold Szondi, son test, sa doctrine*, Brussels: Mardaga, 1974.

23 Guattari, F., *Psychoanalysis and Transversality*, Los Angeles: Semiotext, 2015.

24 Chaigneau, H., "Ce qui suffit. Réflexions surgies de la fréquentation au long cours des schizophrènes", *L'information psychiatrique* 59, no. 3, 1983.

25 The concept of complementary relations was invented by Eugène Dupréel (*Sociologie Générale*, 1948) and used in our practice by Tosquelles.

26 Racamier, P.-C., *Les perversions narcissiques*, Paris: Payot, 1992.

27 Delion, P., *Fonction phorique, holding et institution*, Toulouse: érès, 2018.

28 Resnik, S., *Biographie de l'inconscient*, Paris: Dunod, 2006, p. 17.

29 Freud, S., "Jokes and Their Relation to the Unconscious", *S.E.*, 8, London: Hogarth.

30 Dejours, C., "La psychiatrie résiste-t-elle au néoliberalisme?" (Will Psychiatry Survive Neoliberalism?), *L'information psychiatrique* 93, 2017, pp. 39–42.

31 Delion, P., "La function Balint. Sa place dans l'enseignement et dans la formation psychothérapique et son effet porteur dans la relation soignant-soigné", *VST*, no. 95, 2007, pp. 48–52.

32 Delion, P., "Psychiatrie sécure versus flichiatrie sécuritaire", *Le Carnet PSY*, no. 153, 2011.

33 Delion, P., *La république des faux-selfs* (The Republic of False Selves), Paris: Éditions d'une, 2019.

Closing Remarks

The transferential constellation is the smallest form of institution needed by a patient with an archaic pathology in order to make progress in his psychotherapy. This fundamental element of institutional psychotherapy originates in a rewriting of transference phenomena evaluated in light of these pathologies, which considerably antecede the neuroses. When we speak of a constellation, we speak of a team. But for a psychiatric team, or any other team of medico-social or social work professionals responsible for these pathologies to accomplish its task, its members have to work together to bring about the conditions necessary for implementing this device. Indeed, it is important to remember the history of institutional psychotherapy to understand the reasons that led to its creation, the resistances it encountered and the strategies it had to put in place.

Today, we stand at a critical juncture for the future of psychiatry: either the present orientation becomes even stronger, letting the philosophies of "a priori" work win the day, in which case all our fragile innovations intended to preserve the humanistic dimension of our work will be swept away; or we will be able to continue to rely on "a posteriori" work philosophies as well, and the conditions needed for individual, group and institutional psychotherapies will be preserved. The first form of therapy, "a priori", originates in classic pedagogical models and consists of preparing what will be transmitted, learned and imposed on someone in the position of a learner. Today, the prevalent attitude seems to be that mental illness can respond to rehabilitation, which will compensate for previous disregard of it. A plan of action is drawn up, a program of activities, a recovery protocol, therapeutic training. The "treatment" consists of going through the stages one after the other, and claiming that through perseverance, the desired result has been achieved.

The second form of therapy, "a posteriori", occurs when the caregiver shares an experience with the patient, about what happened, how

DOI: 10.4324/9781003380269-7

to understand it and how to learn something from it that will produce change. The ideology currently in vogue places great hope in the first method, excluding almost systematically the second option, about which it falsely claims that it is not scientifically validated. In truth, it would seem reasonable to use both approaches in a complementary manner, depending on the intended aim. From the pedagogical and educational perspective, the "a priori" method seems useful (although often insufficient) provided it does not become tyrannical. But when what is in question is the method of care, the second approach seems more relevant. Today's debate is biased by the more favorable results, presented as scientific, obtained with the first method; moreover, it is difficult to submit the second method to comparative evaluations. In addition, the fact is that the latter has not sought to research this question sufficiently, since it focuses primarily on the study of individual cases. At present, a number of researchers[1] are doing this work, and longer-term results appear to be comparable, even superior, for the second approach. But although institutional psychotherapy accepts the use of either method depending on the problem concerned, the transferential constellation has to be implemented as part of the second method. The problem is that today's management techniques are firmly rooted in the "a priori" method. And it is certain that today's new management is not moving in a desirable direction.

But the fact is that we have never seen caregivers display a humane attitude towards severely ill patients unless they themselves are treated in a humane fashion by their superiors. One cannot be well-meaning to obey a decree, or generous to follow a protocol. Experience has shown us that without recourse to these indispensable institutional devices, people with archaic pathologies cannot be helped sufficiently to enable them to live with and in the community by relying simply on their own resources and the support of caregivers with whom they have humane relations. In the final analysis, in our field of work we always handcraft,[2] with the patient's help, his made-to-measure therapeutic suit, rather than choosing the easy solution of the ready-made. This is why, until something better comes along, the transferential constellation can constitute a basic form of resistance, effective for patients and generating hope for caregivers.

Notes

1 Thurin, J.-M., "From the Evaluation of Psychotherapies to Research in Psychotherapy and Psychoanalysis", in *Research in Psychoanalysis* 1, no. 23, 2017, pp. 55–68.

2 Venet, E., *Manifeste pour une psychiatrie artisanale*, Lagrasse: Verdier, 2020.

Index

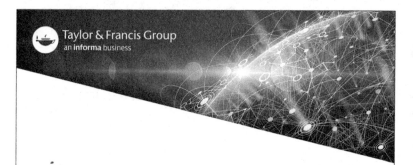

Printed in the United States
by Baker & Taylor Publisher Services